"A bold and enlightening assault against the lack we see in the world. Dr. Cornelius Quek's passion shines through and inspires believers to trust God to provide for our needs, as well as for the resources to support the dreams and assignments He has put in our hearts. What I love about this book is that it's written from a place of experience, so it carries breakthrough and an impartation into an abundant life. Whether you're a missionary, a business person just starting your journey with God, or a veteran who's been walking with Jesus for years, I highly recommend this book as a boost of faith in believing for God's abundance over your life!"

—*Kris Vallotton*
Senior Associate Leader, Bethel Church, Redding, CA
Co-founder, Bethel School of Supernatural Ministry
Author of eleven books, including *The Supernatural Ways of Royalty*,
Heavy Rain, and *Destined to Win*.

"Many believers understand God to be the Provider, but few experience His provision on a consistent basis. In *Provided: The God Who Walks in the Middle of Your Need*, Dr. Cornelius Quek delivers a knockout punch to the spirit of lack in our lives. With sound biblical teaching and practical applications, he shows us how to tap in to the magnanimity of the Father's heart and how to receive His provision for all our needs and for the God-given dreams and destiny for our lives. The work of the kingdom will be accelerated if God's people learn how to access the wealth of His resources. This is a timely prophetic message for the body of Christ!"

—*Ché Ahn*
President, Harvest International Ministry
Founding Pastor, HRock Church, Pasadena, CA
International Chancellor, Wagner University
Author, *The Grace of Giving* and *God Wants to Bless You*

"If you want to learn how much God loves you, and how He operates, *really operates*, in your life and in the lives of your friends and loved ones, this is the book for you. Dr. Cornelius Quek has the unique gift and unparalleled anointing to 'show God to you' through personal stories that demonstrate *who* God really is! You are about to learn how personal God is. I only wish someone had given me this book when I was much younger. *Please*, get this book for yourself today, and get another one for someone you truly care for. Neither of you will be sorry that you did."

—Steve Shultz
Founder, *The Elijah List*

"Dr. Cornelius Quek has truly put together a masterpiece—an outstanding and balanced view of what it means to be living in God's provision. He has skillfully given us the biblical context of covenant provision. God's provision doesn't just involve physical things; it encompasses the total provision of God—body, soul, and spirit. Cornelius emphasizes that provision comes through a healthy understanding and relationship with God our Father. Jesus said that, when we seek first His kingdom and His righteousness, all of these things will be added unto us. I was captivated by how Cornelius painted the picture of God's covenant with mankind and Jesus's parables, making them come alive. I also was touched by the real-life experiences and testimonies included in this book. This book kept my attention from beginning to end."

—*Pastor Kathy Balcombe*
Director, Revival Chinese Ministries International
Pastor, Revival Christian Church
Hong Kong

"Provision is a subject that occupies a massive amount of our time, talent and focus, and one that sits heavily on the heart of every person on earth. Thankfully, the subject of provision is also deeply and continuously on the heart of God. In his new book, Dr. Cornelius Quek presents a fresh approach to this topic that is intensely biblical, spiritually powerful, and uniquely personal. In an age in which much of the teaching on prosperity is superficial and self-centered, it is so refreshing to read a book that is deeply grounded in Scripture, while, at the same time, filled with real-life testimonies that will not only impart mountain-moving faith but also challenge the reader to a deeper intimacy and dependence upon our heavenly Father. This book will change your life!"

—Dr. Michael Brodeur
Founder and consultant, Destiny Finder & Pastor's Coach
Author, *Revival Culture*

"Dr. Cornelius Quek has demonstrated an anointed leadership and ministry in the supernatural realm based on the Word of God for the last twenty years in more than twenty countries. His life is a testimony of God's wonder-working power and supernatural provision in His covenant relationship with God. In *Provided: The God Who Walks in the Middle of Your Need*, Cornelius teaches us about God's sovereign and abundant provision through solid instruction and powerful testimonies. He also points out the importance of stewarding what God has provided for us. As you read this book, may you feed on God's faithfulness and experience His generous heart toward you!"

—Retired Lieutenant General Bey Soo Khiang
Chief of Defense (1995–2000)
Singapore Armed Forces

"My spiritual grandson, Cornelius, has ably captured many precious lessons he has learned in his walk of faith, revealing that our Father God is good and caring. At the same time, he cautions against the get-rich-quick spirit of greed. *Provided: The God Who Walks in the Middle of Your Need* gives us a wonderful framework for growth so that, even if we suffer the loss of all things like Paul, we can continue to be vibrant and minister the words of Philippians 4:19: *"My God will supply all your need according to His riches in glory by Christ Jesus."*

—Most Reverend Dr. Moses Tay
7th Bishop, Anglican Diocese of Singapore (1982–2000)
1st Archbishop, Anglican Province of South East Asia (1996–2000)

"I have known Cornelius since he was a young pastor and leader in Singapore. Over the years, his unwavering and contagious faith in an extraordinary God has catapulted him to accomplish supernatural exploits for the kingdom. Here is a man and a shining example of great courage, influence, and leadership. His ministry is an inspiration to believers, both in the ministry and the marketplace. I highly recommend this book to all who wish to learn to walk by faith in our loving heavenly Father and *Jehovah Jireh*."

—*James Chia*
Group President, Pico Art International
pico.com

"Over the past four years that I have known Cornelius Quek, he has consistently exemplified and promoted a lifestyle of trust in the goodness of God. In *Provided*, Dr. Cornelius presents a sound, biblical understanding of provision and prosperity rooted in dependence on the 'immutable, benevolent, loving' nature of the heavenly Father. It's about trusting God's character—trusting who He is. Readers will find this book immediately applicable, summoning them to new levels of faith, prayer and obedience."

—*Dr. Randy Turpin*
President, Valor Christian College, Columbus, Ohio

PROVIDED

THE GOD WHO WALKS IN THE MIDDLE OF YOUR NEED

DR. CORNELIUS QUEK

WHITAKER
HOUSE

PROVIDED:
The God Who Walks in the Middle of Your Need

Dr. Cornelius Quek
The 7k.org
info@the7k.org

ISBN: 978-1-64123-003-2
eBook ISBN: 978-1-62911-994-6
Printed in the United States of America
© 2018 by Dr. Cornelius Quek

Whitaker House
1030 Hunt Valley Circle
New Kensington, PA 15068
www.whitakerhouse.com

Library of Congress Cataloging-in-Publication Data
LC record available at https://lccn.loc.gov/2017059956

1 2 3 4 5 6 7 8 9 10 11 **WH** 25 24 23 22 21 20 19 18

THIS BOOK IS DEDICATED...

To my late parents: You were the first to show me what provision looked like and felt like. I know this book would make you so proud.

To my wife, Tiffany: You are my best friend, my constant source of love, support, and encouragement. God showed me what a great Provider He is when He gave me you.

To Pastor Bill Johnson and Bethel Church: Thank you for stewarding and hosting the presence of God so well. It is such an honor and joy to serve this house and call Bethel home.

To the outstanding community at Elisha's Room and Destiny House: Doing life as a family with many of you stunning individuals has fueled my passion for the Lord and His kingdom purposes.

To this generation and the generations to come: May you never bow down to the spirit of lack. May you always experience God's gracious provision and accomplish great exploits for His kingdom's sake.

CONTENTS

FOREWORD

Provided is more than a book about living in financial freedom; it is a book that can radically change mind-sets and set people free to step into a more abundant life that Jesus died for us to have. (See John 10:10.) I am so honored to write this foreword for my dear friend Dr. Cornelius Quek. Over the years, I have witnessed the anointing on Cornelius' life to bring breakthrough in the area of finance and stewardship, fulfilling the promises of God.

In the summer of 2013, a woman drove from Oakland to Redding (about three hours) to be a part of our 8 A.M. worship gathering at Destiny House. Toward the end of our meeting, we gathered around her to pray and prophesy over her. Cornelius released his prayers and anointing. A few days later, this woman informed us that $217,544.21 was forgiven off the principal of her home. This is just one of the many testimonies God has released through Cornelius' prayers. I have seen this time and time again.

Cornelius' absolute dependence on God is inspiring. His attitude and reliance upon Him to meet all his needs has never been shaken since I have known him. He has a proven track record of releasing hope and breakthrough in this area. *Provided: The God Who Walks in the Middle of Your Need* is not just a brilliantly written book, it is the core message he lives by every day. So many in my community, including myself, have been incredibly blessed by the authority and anointing he carries and stewards in this area. Cornelius has taught us the significance of operating in the spirit of generosity in times of need.

I remember talking with Cornelius in the beginning stages of development for this book, and one of his early titles for it was something like *Money Is Not the Problem*. This is so true. If we are having problems with money, it is just highlighting a deeper issue we have in our hearts. It is said that, if someone wins the lottery, he will be right back where he started from after awhile because his money habits haven't changed. Millionaires, on the other hand, can go bankrupt and then make another million dollars soon after. Why? Because money was never really the issue. The key is cultivating a healthy perspective of God's goodness, learning to be content in all circumstances, and stewarding what He pours out.

God is good, and He is always for us. We can trust that He wants the best for us and is working behind the scenes on our behalf as we keep our focus on Him. As we do this, we gain courage to step out in faith toward Him even if we don't know what will happen. He longs for us to take our eyes off our circumstances and focus on Him and His greatness. It's important to choose truth over circumstances. This is a shift in belief systems, believing not in what we can see but in the truth of who God says He is. If we really believe God is who He says He is, our faith in Him will never waiver.

When we see things in the right perspective and believe His truth, we won't question whether He will provide for our needs. (See Philippians 4:19.) How am I going to pay rent this month? How am I ever going to get out of debt? Will I ever get to go on my dream vacation? These challenges all have their answer in Jesus, who is the way, the truth, and the life. (See John 14:6.) Jesus is the answer to every problem and issue we face. He will lead us and give us solutions as we seek Him first.

When we posture our hearts to believe the truth that God will take care of us just as He does the birds of the air, we won't need to worry about Him meeting our immediate needs again. (See Matthew 6:25–34.) Perspective is everything. Is our faith in Jesus and His promises or in what we can see? Do we believe the promise of Philippians 1:6, that God will complete what He starts? If God makes a promise, we can trust that He will fulfill it. This may not come in our timing or the way we think, but if God has revealed to us a promise, then we can put all our hope and trust in Him.

If we can learn to keep our eyes on Jesus and worship Him in all circumstances, we will go to new heights and new depths with Him. We will enter into His gates with thanksgiving and praise in our hearts in all circumstances. (See Psalm 100:4–5.) That's the secret that Paul discovered. (See Philippians 4:12–13.) He learned how to let God direct His steps and source his happiness. God is the source of our hope and joy; nothing, not even lack, can steal that away.

I have learned that the enemy uses lack to make us depressed, whereas God uses lack to propel us into more of Him. We can allow our roots to grow deeper in Him and build a solid foundation, so that, when abundance comes, we are strong enough to steward and channel it to be a blessing to those around us. When we experience lack or a spirit of fear, that's the time to take on the opposite spirit. Ask God what He is really up to and worship more exuberantly, focusing on Him. In seasons of lack, dream bigger dreams, and worship, praise, and adore God even more. That may be the only time you have to offer a sacrifice of praise in during that situation, and what a gift that is! We can trust that, as we worship Him for His faithfulness, even in times of lack, He will open up the heavens on our behalf. (See 2 Chronicles 20.)

No matter what season you find yourself in, I believe that God will use this book to unlock greater faith in Him and a healthy perspective to steward what He provides for you. God is faithful, and He is always for you. May God rewire your brain with heavenly pathways and the right perspective so that your foundation is in God alone and you remain unshakeable no matter what storms come and go. I pray that, as you read *Provided: The God Who Walks in the Middle of Your Need*, you will receive a massive revelation of the Father's unrelenting love, recognizing that He has already gone to all extremes to demonstrate His love for you. May you be marked by His love so much that you will never again question His goodness. May the truth that He is your faithful Provider fill you with fresh hope and expectation for the abundant life He's already given in Jesus. Blessings and fire be upon your life as you read this gift.

—*Dr. Jennifer A. Miskov*
Founding Director, Destiny House
Redding, California
Author, *Walking on Water: Experiencing a Life of Miracles, Courageous Faith & Union with God*

INTRODUCTION: IT'S A DONE DEAL!

College days were rough. Ramen was my best friend, not just because I am Asian, but because money was a rare commodity in that season of my life. Clean clothing was also not very common unless I managed to scramble ten quarters by the end of the week—five for a wash, five for a dry. I remember one of those days when I gathered my mountain of dirty laundry and made my way to the laundromat. I took five steps out of my dorm room when it hit me like a ton of bricks: I had only seventy-five cents to my name; how was I going to do my laundry?

A moment of stark reality, a sigh of disappointment, and five retracted steps later, I was back in my dorm room. I remembered praying, "Lord, if you can send ravens to feed Elijah, surely you can give me clean clothes." I went about my day. Later that evening, I was at church, and James, a homeless guy I had met the week before, walked up to me.

"I don't know why I am doing this, but here's a dollar for you." James stretched out his hand toward me.

I was lost for words.

James walked up to me a second time that evening, this time digging deep into his jean pocket. "Now, I really don't know why I am doing this, but here's another dollar for you," he said, handing me four quarters.

"James, I really do appreciate this, but you really don't have to do this."

"You don't understand. I have to," James insisted.

I was dumbfounded but profoundly uplifted. It took awhile to sink in. Besides feeling immense gratitude, I must say the prospect of clean-smelling clothes excited me greatly. That night, the Holy Spirit spoke to me in a matter-of-fact tone: *Son, I am your Source. Look to Me and trust Me. If I decide to hang money on the tree and have you pluck it down, so be it.* I will never forget those words. God was making it plain to me that He is the Source of all provision, whether through supernatural or natural means. The lesson I learned that night has shaped me and spurred me on in my journey of trusting God for His provision in my life. Now it's my turn to encourage you.

Jesus and Paul made two audacious statements concerning God's provision. Jesus promised, *"Seek first the kingdom of God...and all these things will be added to you"* (Matthew 6:33 ESV). Elsewhere, Paul confidently declared, *"My God shall supply all your need according to His riches in glory"* (Philippians 4:19).

This is what I would have said to them: "Jesus, Paul, you can't make statements like that and not be able to back them up!"

I can just imagine Jesus and Paul fist-pumping and shouting with sheer gusto and conviction, "It's a done deal! Don't you worry about it! God will provide for you!" Either Jesus and Paul are right on the money, or they have gone off the deep end. Nevertheless, I thought, *They know God's provision to be a fact when many others think of it only as a good idea. They seem to perceive God's provision as heaven's reality rather than heaven's reluctance.* I believe Jesus and Paul didn't make those bold statements to tease us or to frustrate us. God's provision isn't just a good idea—it's His most gracious promise.

Divine provision is a prerogative of God's children. As a good Father, He delights in providing for us, and He created us with an innate dependency on Him to meet our needs. God is a creative Provider, and He provides through different means. We can't put Him in a box. He can provide through people, a job, a brilliant business idea, or another dramatic fashion. Trusting God for provision tends to make people feel nervous and uneasy. Many feel inadequate in approaching God for provision. They view provision more like a problem rather than a promise from God. They hang on to their inadequacy to trust God rather than God's profound ability to provide. It stirs up more questions than answers. How will God provide? Can God be trusted? How does faith work? What if I don't have faith? What if God doesn't show up? What if—the questions linger. They pray. They believe. They want to believe. And they bite their nails. Trusting in the unknown is scary. Not being in control is disconcerting. There's always going to be a level of discomfort in trusting God for provision. It always requires us to relinquish our fears and control and step out in faith. Ask Abraham, Isaac, Jacob, Joseph, Moses, David, and the other biblical heroes of faith. They all have understood the process well. I believe that if they could give us a word of encouragement, they would concertedly say, "Yes, it is nerve-racking. Yes, it is scary. Yes, it is uncomfortable, but God is able. Understand that to position yourself to receive breakthrough and provision, the promises of God must outweigh your discomfort and fears. You must be acquainted with the promises more than the problems. The issue isn't God's ability to provide for you; it's enlarging your capacity to trust and receive. So, learn to trust and receive. Fix your eyes on Him. God has promised to provide for you. Rest assured!"

The premise of this book is the core belief that God wants and is able to provide for our needs, as well as provide the resources for the God-given dreams and assignments He has called each one of us to. The central theme in the Bible is covenant provision, which is stamped on many narratives in the Bible, beginning with creation all the way to the cross. It is God's gracious inheritance for His children. We enter in to covenant relationship with the Father the moment we are adopted as His sons and daughters. We no longer have to fend for ourselves; the good Father provides and takes care of us.

In teaching the disciples to pray, Jesus said,

Your Father knows the things you have need of before you ask
Him. In this manner, therefore, pray: Our Father in heaven...
give us this day our daily bread.   (Matthew 6:8–9, 11)

Jesus invites us to covenant relationship with the Father with the promise of covenant provision.

I have struggled to find an adequate title for this book. I finally settled on *Provided*. Here's why: It describes the act of provision in the past tense. It is a completed action; it's a done deal. God has made a covenant and established a bond to always supply and care for His children. Although God's covenant provision includes other aspects of our lives, such as health, peace, wisdom, protection, and so forth, I focused on God's provision for our material and financial needs. My goal in this book is to point you to the covenant Provider, Jehovah Jireh, the All-Sufficient One. That is the foundation on which this book was written. This book is by no means an exhaustive treatise on divine providence or finances. Authors like Dave Ramsey, Ron Blue, and Larry Burkett have valuable literature and resources on financial strategies and money management written from a Christian and kingdom perspective.

In this book, you will learn biblical principles and receive keys to help you unlock and access what heaven has already made provision for. The testimonies and prayer declarations in each chapter will build your faith, inspire hope, and guide you in prophesying to your circumstances.

This book was written for the college student trusting God for college expenses, the single mom wondering how she is going to provide for her child, the businessman with a new business venture, the individual preparing for a career in ministry, and all dreamers who wonder how their dreams will ever come to pass.

God is able.

May your life be marked by His covenant faithfulness and radical provision. May you accomplish every God-given assignment and fulfill the destiny He has placed on your life. And may you come to understand the heart of the Father, who greatly delights in providing for His children. His love for you is relentless!

Your fellow sojourner,
Dr. Cornelius Quek

1

"MAY I BE CURSED IF I DO NOT PROVIDE FOR YOU!"

> "It is ridiculous and absurd to think that the God who called you to His assignments would sabotage His plans by shortchanging His provision for you."
> —Cornelius Quek

In a moment of desperation, I found myself bargaining with the Lord and laying my cards on the table: "Father, I am not asking for much, but if You promise to always take care of my basic needs—food on the table, a roof over my head, a job, a family with a wife and children—I promise to lay down my life to serve You for the rest of my days."

"Lord, I know You've called me to make a difference in this world. You have put dreams and aspirations in my heart that are going to require Your provision to be fulfilled. I can't afford to negotiate with lack in my life!"

In the gentlest way, I heard Him say, *Son, it's a deal. Let Me take you on a journey. Turn to Genesis 15. Let Me show you something.*

After these things the word of the LORD came to Abram in a vision, saying, "Do not be afraid, Abram. I am your shield, your exceedingly great reward." But Abram said, "Lord GOD, what will You give me, seeing I go childless, and the heir of my house

is Eliezer of Damascus?" Then Abram said, "Look, You have
given me no offspring; indeed one born in my house is my heir!"
And behold, the word of the LORD came to him, saying, "This
one shall not be your heir, but one who will come from your own
body shall be your heir." Then He brought him outside and said,
"Look now toward heaven, and count the stars if you are able to
number them." And He said to him, "So shall your descendants
be." And he believed in the LORD, and He accounted it to him
for righteousness. Then He said to him, "I am the LORD, who
brought you out of Ur of the Chaldeans, to give you this land to
inherit it." And he said, "Lord GOD, how shall I know that I will
inherit it?" So He said to him, "Bring Me a three-year-old heifer,
a three-year-old female goat, a three-year-old ram, a turtledove,
and a young pigeon." Then he brought all these to Him and cut
them in two, down the middle, and placed each piece opposite the
other; but he did not cut the birds in two. And when the vultures
came down on the carcasses, Abram drove them away. Now
when the sun was going down, a deep sleep fell upon Abram;
and behold, horror and great darkness fell upon him. Then He
said to Abram: "Know certainly that your descendants will be
strangers in a land that is not theirs, and will serve them, and
they will afflict them four hundred years. And also the nation
whom they serve I will judge; afterward they shall come out with
great possessions. Now as for you, you shall go to your fathers in
peace; you shall be buried at a good old age. But in the fourth generation they shall return here, for the iniquity of the Amorites is
not yet complete." And it came to pass, when the sun went down
and it was dark, that behold, there appeared a smoking oven and
a burning torch that passed between those pieces. On the same
day the LORD made a covenant with Abram, saying: "To your
descendants I have given this land, from the river of Egypt to the
great river, the River Euphrates—the Kenites, the Kenezzites,
the Kadmonites, the Hittites, the Perizzites, the Rephaim, the
Amorites, the Canaanites, the Girgashites, and the Jebusites."

(Genesis 15:1–21)

CAN GOD BE TRUSTED?

Since the garden of Eden, Satan's predictable strategy has always been to tempt us to doubt the character and the goodness of God. With this archetypical scheme, he deceived Eve: "Did God really say…? Does God have your best interest at heart? Is He able to provide for you? Is He going to leave you to fend for yourself? Will God keep His promises?" The heart of Genesis 15 begs the question "Will Abram trust in Yahweh?" And, of weighty significance, "Can Yahweh, in fact, be trusted?"

Earlier, in Genesis 12 and 13, God repeatedly promised Abram descendants and land. (See Genesis 12:2–3, 7; 13:14–17.) It's starting to sound like a broken record. Abram was seventy-five years old, and Sarah was barren. We arrive at chapter 15, and the barrenness lingers. The chapter begins brightly with God assuring Abram that He would be his Protector and Rewarder.

> After these things the word of the LORD came to Abram in a vision, saying, "Do not be afraid, Abram. I am your shield, your exceedingly great reward." (Genesis 15:1)

However, I imagine that, for Abram, these words would pale in comparison to his current situation of childlessness. Words and promises of someday possessing land would fall to the ground, futile and conflicting with the current state of landlessness. Abram is confronted with his ability to muster up enough faith to trust in God. Will he be able to trust God? Can God be trusted? Will God trust Abram? These are crucial questions, and their answers would alter the history of Israel and God's people for eternity. How will Abram continue to completely trust in the promises of God when all the surrounding evidence shouted impossibility? Childlessness was viewed as an outright disaster in the ancient world, bearing social and cultural contempt. Without children, no one could carry on Abram's family line (you and I may not exist!). If nothing happened, Abram was going to take matters into his own hands and adopt Eliezer, a servant in his household, as his heir.

> *But Abram said, "Lord God, what will You give me, seeing I go*
> *childless, and the heir of my house is Eliezer of Damascus?" Then*
> *Abram said, "Look, You have given me no offspring; indeed one*
> *born in my house is my heir!"*   (Genesis 15:2–3)

God reassured Abram that he would have a child of his own.
For the first time, God showed Abram the stars in the skies, and it
was a sign to him that his descendants would be equally incalculable. (See Genesis 15:4–5.) In the pitch darkness of the Near Eastern
night, Abram lifted his head and gazed at the constellations of stars.
I imagine his eyes glistening with hope and his faith being stirred as
he attempted to count them one by one. Abram accepted this con-
firmation concerning his progeny, albeit, deep inside, questions and
uncertainty regarding possession of land may still have lingered.

"CUT UP THE ANIMALS!"

Having faith in God does not rule out questions. Abram believed
God, and it was accounted to him as righteousness (see Genesis 15:6),
but it didn't stop him from asking God a legitimate question: *"Lord
God, how shall I know that I will inherit* [the land]*?"* (Genesis 15:8).
God's response to his query hardly seemed inspiring or comforting.
It appeared so random and inconsequential.

> *So He said to him, "Bring Me a three-year-old heifer, a three-*
> *year-old female goat, a three-year-old ram, a turtledove, and a*
> *young pigeon." Then he brought all these to Him and cut them in*
> *two, down the middle, and placed each piece opposite the other;*
> *but he did not cut the birds in two.*   (Genesis 15:9–10)

Remarkably, Abram seemed to understand exactly what the
Lord was asking him to do. God was giving him instructions to prepare a "covenant cutting" ceremony. Abram proceeded to gather the
animals, cut and separated them in two, and placed them in front of
Him. The day had gone by, and the sun was going down. Abram fell
into a deep sleep. As the night approached, all of heaven awaited in
silent and eager anticipation to see what Yahweh would do next.

The evening quieted and, when it would seem like all that remained was the deathly passage of animals, suddenly, a glowing fire emerged from the darkness of night. The scene took a dramatic shift with a theophany, a manifestation of God, complete with pyro-technics. A smoking firepot with a flaming torch amazingly glided between the pieces of the animals. Fire in the Bible is often symbolic of the abiding presence of God. In this riveting encounter, Yahweh, in His Shekinah glory, represented by fiery symbols, passed between the rows of animal flesh to seal His covenant with Abram. It was a stunning display of His power and magnificence!

> *And it came to pass, when the sun went down and it was dark, that behold, there appeared a smoking oven and a burning torch that passed between those pieces. On the same day the LORD made a covenant with Abram, saying: "To your descendants I have given this land, from the river of Egypt to the great river, the River Euphrates."*   (Genesis 15:17)

In Hebrew literature, the central narrative of Genesis 15 is known as *brit bein habetarim*, meaning, "covenant between the pieces." The Hebrew term for covenant making is *karat berit*, literally, "to cut a covenant." (See Genesis 15:18.)[1]

Ritual practices in the ancient Near East offer extensive evidence that animals were slaughtered and cut in half in treaty contraction ceremonies. A "suzerainty treaty" was a Hittite practice in the six-teenth to thirteenth centuries B.C. Suzerains were ancient kings who imposed their covenant treaties on lesser kings, called vassals.[2] In this treaty, the vassal, or the inferior party, would walk between the bleeding pieces of the split animals. He would take an oath of loyalty to his superior, the suzerain: "May the gods do so to me as I have done to these animals if I do not fulfill the terms of this covenant!"[3] A similar biblical reference is found in Jeremiah:

> *And I will give the men who have transgressed My covenant, who have not performed the words of the covenant which they made before Me, when they cut the calf in two and passed between the*

parts of it—the princes of Judah, the princes of Jerusalem, the eunuchs, the priests, and all the people of the land who passed between the parts of the calf—I will give them into the hand of their enemies and into the hand of those who seek their life. Their dead bodies shall be for meat for the birds of the heaven and the beasts of the earth. (Jeremiah 34:18–20)

Although it may seem morbid, the symbolism here is startling. If one were to violate the terms of the covenant, he would perish just like the animals. It was self-maledictory. In other words, to walk between the carcasses is to submit oneself to the fate of the slaughtered animals as a curse and penalty for breaking the covenant.

In Abram's climactic encounter with God's presence, the glowing furnace slowly glided through the animal parts that glistened in the night. Surely the reverential fear of the Lord fell on that place as this holy scene played out. Astonishingly, as Abram stood there rooted and stunned by His glory, he realized he had not been asked to join in the ritual—to pass between the pieces with God. God, in His divine initiative, moved between the cut-up animal parts all by Himself!

> ## THAT GOD WOULD CURSE HIMSELF AND DIE IS INCONCEIVABLE! AND YET THAT'S EXACTLY WHAT HE DID! ALMOST TWO THOUSAND YEARS LATER, GOD CAME IN THE FLESH AND JESUS BECAME A CURSE ON OUR BEHALF. IT WAS THE DIVINE SCANDAL OF ALL ETERNITY!

What was going on? God acted on His own accord, and it was an unconditional, unilateral covenant. He was solely responsible for its fulfillment. God, with astounding authority, was symbolizing that if He were to break His word, He would be sundered just like the butchered animals. It would be tantamount to a curse, a divine self-imprecation, a guarantee that Abram's descendants would inherit and possess the land, or God Himself would die![4] What a scandal that would be! That God would curse Himself and die is inconceivable! And yet that's exactly what He did! Almost two thousand years later, God came in the flesh and Jesus became a curse on our behalf. It was the divine scandal of all eternity! What a God and Savior! Here in Genesis 15, in one act of divine magnanimity, Yahweh took an oath, and in passing between the animal pieces, He irrevocably pledged to fulfill His covenant promise to Abram.

An important aspect of cutting a covenant involves the role of a witness. (See Genesis 31:44–49; Deuteronomy 31:19; Joshua 24:27.) As the new generation of Israelites was poised to enter the Promised Land, Moses called to remembrance their unique covenant with God. He called two witnesses to verify the ratification of the covenant:

> I call heaven and earth as witnesses today against you, that I have set before you life and death, blessing and cursing; therefore choose life, that both you and your descendants may live.
> (Deuteronomy 30:19)

Treaties often conclude with a call for witnesses to confirm the terms of the covenant. Witnesses testify that a covenant has been made and is binding, including the penalty for not honoring the terms of the covenant. In ancient Near Eastern legal transactions, the witnesses were typically the distinctive deities of the parties involved.[5] And since there is no other god but Yahweh in Israel's faith, the created order, heaven and earth, was summoned to testify to the reality of His offer and the reliability of His promise. Creation was called upon as a witness in other instances in the Old Testament, when the Lord entered into some form of legal encounter with the Israelites. (See Deuteronomy 4:26; 31:28; 32:1; Isaiah 1:2; Micah 1:2).

Moreover, God came down in His glory to inaugurate a formal covenant with Abram. And since He could swear by none greater, He swore by Himself. The Lord took an oath, sanctioning Himself for Abram's benefit.

> For example, there was God's promise to Abraham. Since there was no one greater to swear by, God took an oath in his own

name, saying: "I will certainly bless you, and I will multiply your descendants beyond number." Then Abraham waited patiently, and he received what God had promised. Now when people take an oath, they call on someone greater than themselves to hold them to it. And without any question that oath is binding. God also bound himself with an oath, so that those who received the promise could be perfectly sure that he would never change his mind. So God has given both his promise and his oath. These two things are unchangeable because it is impossible for God to lie. (Hebrews 6:13–18 NLT)

God put His name and reputation on the line. He named Himself the guarantor of His word. In swearing by Himself, God is bound to His word by His character. He is incapable of dishonoring His own name and reputation. Now, Abram can be confident that God's promises were forever sure. He will provide! Later, in Genesis 17:5, God changed Abram's name, which means "exalted father," to Abraham, the "father of a multitude!"[6] The goodness of God was the motivating force, bringing all His promises to Abram to fruition, substantiated by His name. His name is El Shaddai—God Almighty, the All-Sufficient One, the God who is more than enough! God's zeal and commitment to providing for Abram are backed up with the resources of heaven!

THE COVENANT OF GRACE

Since Abram did not walk through the pieces, he was not obligated to realize God's promises, only to live in obedience to God, believe by faith, and receive His promises. It was a unilateral covenant. Abram was a recipient, not a contributor, to the covenant. He was not expected to offer promissory elements to the bond; he was to accept it as offered, keep it as demanded, and receive the results that God, by oath, assured would not be withheld.

When Abram was ninety-nine years old, the LORD appeared to Abram and said to him, "I am Almighty God; walk before Me and be blameless. And I will make My covenant between Me and you, and will multiply you exceedingly." (Genesis 17:1–2)

When God affirmed His covenant with Abram, God instructed him to *"walk before* [Him] *and be blameless."* Living under God's covenantal blessings and provision is a privilege as God's children. However, it requires us to live responsibly, in covenant obedience to God and His ways. The covenant of grace does not condone licentious and irresponsible living.

> LIVING UNDER GOD'S COVENANTAL BLESSINGS AND PROVISION IS A PRIVILEGE AS GOD'S CHILDREN. HOWEVER, IT REQUIRES US TO LIVE RESPONSIBLY, IN COVENANT OBEDIENCE TO GOD AND HIS WAYS.

God's covenant with Abram was a covenant of grace. God Himself will provide. We are incapable, even on our best days, of earning His blessings. They are a gift from God. We don't deserve them. He graciously lavishes them on us. We receive them by faith and obedience to God's Word and promises. What a selfless and munificent heavenly Father we have!

WE ARE A BLESSED PEOPLE

Another significant feature of the suzerainty treaty was what was known as successional arrangements.[7] These are arrangements and provisions set in place for the continuity of the covenant relationship over future generations. In other words, the terms that have been promised by the vassal (that is, God) to the suzerain (that is, Abram) are binding to the suzerain's successors and heirs as well.

> *You are sons of the prophets, and of the covenant which God made with our fathers, saying to Abraham, "And in your seed all the families of the earth shall be blessed."* (Acts 3:25)

Here's the implication: We are descendants of Abraham. We have become sons and daughters, heirs and successors to the covenant that God established with Abraham. What has been promised to him is promised to us, as well. The blessings and benefits are continuous. We are a blessed people!

This dramatic act of covenant making prefigures the precious gift of God's own Son. God's covenant with Abraham took on new life in Christ, the Promised One in whom *"all the families of the earth shall be blessed."* We have now become recipients of God's blessings through the seed of Abraham, Jesus Christ. Isn't it so like God to sacrifice so that His inheritance—His sons and daughters—might gain? Because of Jesus, we have been positioned to receive all things from the Father. Joy, peace, righteousness, hope, protection, deliverance, grace, favor, divine health, financial and material provision, and so much more have become our inheritance.

> *He who did not spare His own Son, but delivered Him up for us all, how shall He not with Him also freely give us all things?*
>
> (Romans 8:32)

Iain Duguid puts it beautifully:

> By what figure could God have demonstrated his commitment more graphically to Abram? How could it have been displayed more vividly? The only way would have been for the figure to become a reality, for the ever living God to take on human nature and taste death in the place of the covenant-breaking children of Abram. And that is precisely what God did in Jesus Christ. On the cross, the covenant curse fell completely on Jesus, so that the guilty ones who place their trust in him might experience the blessings of the covenant. Jesus bore the punishment for our sins, so that God might be our God and we might be his people.[8]

I believe the apostle Paul understood this fully when he penned this confident promise in Philippians: *"And this same God who takes care of me will supply all your needs from his glorious riches, which have been given to us in Christ Jesus"* (Philippians 4:19 NLT).

"SON, I AM CUTTING A COVENANT WITH YOU!"

At the beginning of the chapter, I recounted a decisive moment when I laid out my cards on the table before the Lord, desperately wanting to know if He would promise to take care of all my needs if I choose to serve Him the rest of my life. As He revealed to me the significance and the weight of His covenant with Abram, the Holy Spirit said to me, *Son, it is a deal. Today, I'm cutting a covenant with you, just like I did with Abraham. I will walk past your request and needs as you laid them out before me just as I walked past Abram's cut animals. Today you will know that I will always provide for all your needs. I am your Covenant-Keeper.*

These reassuring words reverberated within the walls of my heart. God has kept His promise and continues to do so. He is forever faithful! He's that good!

> *Understand, therefore, that the LORD your God is indeed God. He is the faithful God who keeps his covenant for a thousand generations and lavishes his unfailing love on those who love him and obey his commands.* (Deuteronomy 7:9 NLT)

PRAYER OF FAITH

In this book, I would like to release a prayer of faith over you. As you pursue His will for your life and trust Him to supply all your needs, may you encounter El Shaddai, the All-Sufficient One, and experience His covenant provision. As a prophetic act, extend your arms, which is symbolic of two lines of cut animals. I want you to imagine placing all your needs into your hands. Now, ask the Lord to release His presence and walk in between your arms and your needs. Pray this with me:

> Father, thank You that You are the covenant-keeping God. Just as You cut a covenant with Abram, I ask You today to cut a covenant with me. Lord, my desire is to do Your will. You will provide for those You love. I lay my needs before You; would You walk past them and release Your presence

and Your provision. From this day forth, I declare that I will never be in lack. Lord, I declare that heaven's resources, including finances, be poured out over my life. Thank You, Father, that You shall supply all my needs according to Your riches in glory in Christ Jesus. Hallelujah! In Jesus's name, I pray. Amen!

GOD'S RIGHT HAND OF PROVISION

"You will show me the path of life; in Your presence is fullness
of joy; at Your right hand are pleasures forevermore."
—Psalm 16:11

Cornelius, how are you doing with your finances?" asked one of the staff members.

I had just begun the Discipleship Training School program at Youth with a Mission Singapore in 1998. That morning, I woke up with $2.70 to my name, tucked away in my wallet. I needed $1.50 to buy a train ticket to get to class and the same amount to get home afterward.

I remembered praying, *Lord, I have money to get to class, and all I need is thirty cents to get home. I don't care about lunch. I just want to be able to get home.*

I replied cordially to the staff member, "I just need thirty cents to buy a train ticket to get home today."

She smiled but did not say a word. I returned the smile politely but, in my heart, candidly thought, *Why would you ask me about my needs but just smile and not do anything to help?* I went about the day and sat through my classes.

We broke for lunch, and another staff member came up to me and said, "Cornelius, let me take you out for lunch."

Hmm—maybe, just maybe—God would give me thirty cents by the end of the day.

We proceeded to lunch, ate a nice meal, and enjoyed a good catch up. We were getting ready to leave when the staff member stopped me in my tracks and said, "Cornelius, give me your right hand."

Not really knowing what to expect, I extended my right hand, and she placed $50 in it. I must admit, I knew God could provide thirty cents, but what would I do now with $49.70 extra? Excellent problem!

"IF YOU DON'T PROVIDE, I AM WALKING TO CHURCH"

A few weeks later, as part of our weekly intercession time, a group of us went to a local university to prayer walk around the campus. That morning, I had let God know how my wallet was doing: *Here we go again, Lord,* I thought. *I have money to make it to the prayer site and back. I don't care about lunch. All I care about is that I have money to take the bus to church tomorrow morning to lead worship. If You don't provide, I am walking to church.*

I had to be at church at 8:00 A.M. in the morning, and I figured it would take me about three hours to walk there, which meant I had to start walking at 5:00 A.M. Really, I didn't have the luxury of options, but I was determined to get to church on time.

I went on the prayer walk with two other students. Afterward, one of them offered to buy me lunch, which I gladly accepted. I was beginning to think God cared about lunches. I hopped on the train with my friend, Su Jin, and discovered that her destination was two stops after mine. We were chatting about our time at YWAM when she asked me, "Cornelius, how are you doing with your finances?"

You can't help but be somewhat thrilled when someone asks you a question like that. I kept a straight face, and there might even have been a melodramatic tone in my reply, "I am leading worship at church tomorrow morning. If God doesn't provide, I am going to start walking at 5 A.M. to get there by 8 A.M."

"Cornelius, God is faithful. He will provide for you," she replied sympathetically.

I smiled heartily and said, "Amen," thinking, *Thanks for the very spiritual answer but…?*

Here we go again.

The train bell rang at my stop. I alighted and bid farewell to Su Jin. Dragging my steps to the ticketing machine, I debated with the Lord (all right, it was a complaint session) why He didn't have Su Jin do something about my financial situation. My steps felt heavier as I thought about my long and arduous early morning walk to church the next day. Just as I slid my ticket into the ticketing machine, I heard someone shout my name.

"Cornelius, wait up!"

It was Su Jin. She had gotten off the train and was running toward me. We were standing on either side of the ticketing machine, and she said, "Cornelius, give me your right hand."

Then she slid $10 into my hand. It may seem like a small amount, but God's ability to know when and how to provide is extraordinary. His knowledge is infinite, and His timing is immaculate.

> *These all wait for You, that You may give them their food in due season. What You give them they gather in; You open Your hand, they are filled with good.*   (Psalm 104:27–28)

THE RIGHT HAND OF GOD

You may have noticed that these two accounts of God's provision came with the same invitation: "Cornelius, give me your right hand." It wasn't coincidental. I believe the Lord intended to teach me something, so I started searching Scriptures referencing God's right hand, and the Holy Spirit began to instruct me about its significance.

The right hand of God is understood as the place of salvation (see Psalm 44:3, 138:7, 17:7), victory (see Psalm 98:1, 118:15–16, 110:1), royalty (see Psalm 45:9), authority and power (see 1 Peter 3:22;

Mark 14:62, 16:19), safety and security (see Psalm 73:23, 139:10; Isaiah 41:10, 13), intercession (see Romans 8:34; Hebrews 7:25), and honor and blessing (see Matthew 25:33; Hebrews 1:3; Genesis 48:17).

Psalm 16 is filled with hope, promising us confidence and security in God's provision:

> O Lord, You are the portion of my inheritance and my cup; You maintain my lot. The lines have fallen to me in pleasant places; yes, I have a good inheritance.   (verses 5–6)

> I have set the Lord always before me; because He is at my right hand I shall not be moved.   (verse 8)

> You will show me the path of life; in Your presence is fullness of joy; at Your right hand are pleasures forevermore.   (verse 11)

The psalmist used the words *"portion of my inheritance," "my cup," "my lot," "lines have fallen in pleasant places,"* and *"good inheritance"* (verses 5–6) to powerfully reflect that Yahweh allots the land to whomever He wills. Moreover, He provides for its security and prosperity. The psalmist understood that Yahweh, not any foreign idols, is the Source and Provider of all good things.

> I say to the Lord, "You are my Lord; apart from you I have no good thing."   (Psalm 16:2 NIV)

Verses 8 and 11 of Psalm 16 refer to God's mighty *"right hand."* Because of His right hand, we *"shall not be moved"* (verse 8), and we can be confident in His ability to provide *"pleasures forevermore"* (verse 11).

THE FAVORABLE POSITION FOR GREATER BLESSING

According to the ancient Near East tradition, one of the purposes of the laying on of hands was to impart a blessing. It was first recorded in the Bible in Genesis 48, when Jacob conferred the blessing upon Ephraim and Manasseh. In that culture, the law of primogeniture states that the elder son would receive the greater blessing.

Now when Joseph saw that his father laid his right hand on the head of Ephraim, it displeased him; so he took hold of his father's hand to remove it from Ephraim's head to Manasseh's head. And Joseph said to his father, "Not so, my father, for this one is the firstborn; put your right hand on his head."
(Genesis 48:17–18)

Jacob placed his right hand on Joseph's eldest son. His right hand was the hand and the position by which the greater anointing, favor, and blessing was imparted to the firstborn. As Christ is the *"firstborn among many brethren"* (Romans 8:29), so we are "firstborn" spiritually (see Hebrews 12:23). The Lord has extended His right hand toward us, and we are blessed and highly favored!

"HAS THE LORD'S ARM BEEN SHORTENED?"

The people of Israel complained to Moses about their plight and the lack of quality food, specifically meat. They were getting tired of eating manna. They had exhausted all kinds of ways to cook manna. They ground it, beat it, cooked it in pans, and even made them into cakes; they'd had enough.

So the children of Israel also wept again and said: "Who will give us meat to eat? We remember the fish which we ate freely in Egypt, the cucumbers, the melons, the leeks, the onions, and the garlic; but now our whole being is dried up; there is nothing at all except this manna before our eyes!"   (Numbers 11:4–6)

Although the Lord was displeased with their complaint, He promised to provide them with meat for an entire month. That is a lot of meat for six hundred thousand men! Moses was skeptical and questioned the Lord.

Moses said, "The people whom I am among are six hundred thousand men on foot; yet You have said, 'I will give them meat, that they may eat for a whole month.' Shall flocks and herds be slaughtered for them, to provide enough for them? Or shall all the fish of the sea be gathered together for them, to provide enough for them?" And the LORD said to Moses, "Has the LORD's arm been shortened? Now you shall see whether what I say will happen to you or not."　　　　　　　　　　(Numbers 11:21–23)

It sounded like God had been stirred in His reply. "Moses, open your eyes really big! Watch what I'm about to do, you turkey! My arm is longer than you think!" Jokes aside, we are not to underestimate the power of God's hand to provide for us. It is an insult to His ability.

Ah, Lord GOD! Behold, You have made the heavens and the earth by Your great power and outstretched arm. There is nothing too hard for You.　　　　　　　　　　(Jeremiah 32:17)

THE PRAYER OF JABEZ

Now Jabez was more honorable than his brothers, and his mother called his name Jabez, saying, "Because I bore him in pain." And Jabez called on the God of Israel saying, "Oh, that You would bless me indeed, and enlarge my territory, that Your hand would be with me, and that You would keep me from evil, that I may not cause pain!" So God granted him what he requested.
　　　　　　　　　　(1 Chronicles 4:9–10)

Little is known about Jabez other than what is shared in these verses about his birth and prayer. Jabez's prayer is anything but little. It's big, bold, and bad (in a really good way). Things did not get off to a promising start for Jabez, who no one had ever heard of, although he was deemed more honorable than his brothers. Jabez's story began with his name. His mother called him "Jabez," because she *"bore him in pain."* In Hebrew, the word *Jabez* is associated with "pain" and a literal rendering of his name could read, "He causes (or will cause) pain."[1] I am thankful my parents didn't name me Nuisance Annoying Quek.

All babies are born with some degree of pain. However, something was unusual about the birth of Jabez, to the extent that his mother chose an unfortunate and regretful name for him. Perhaps the circumstances surrounding his birth were traumatic. Maybe she had a prolonged labor. Perhaps the mother's emotional pain was overwhelming. Maybe the stress and burden of feeding another mouth caused much uncertainty and panic. No matter what caused her pain, her choice of a name for Jabez indicated it wasn't a fun situation.

Jabez grew up with a name every boy would love to hate. An ancient belief concerning a person's name was that it represented that individual's character or personal destiny and calling. A name was often taken as a wish for, or prophecy about, a child's future. No one would fault Jabez for praying to God that His hand would be with him, that He would overturn any curse associated with his name into blessing, that God would alter his destiny from one of pain, harm, and lack to one of favor, protection, and provision. Jabez requested four things—two focused on physical circumstances (expanded territory and freedom from pain) and two on his relationship with God (blessing and God's protective hand). The theme of effective and answered prayers runs through Chronicles. (See 1 Chronicles 5:20–22; 2 Chronicles 20:6–12.) Jabez would have grown up hearing about the deliverance, signs, wonders, and miraculous provisions God had performed on behalf of Israel. By the time he became an adult, he would have known and believed in God's power to deliver, provide for, and bless the children of Israel. Jabez knew God hears and answers specific requests.

So, he prayed, and boy did he pray! He uttered what I call a prodigious prayer, the kind that arrests the attention of heaven. I am a big fan of Jabez's audacious faith. This dude is radical. In Hebrew writing, the addition of *"indeed"* to this prayer reflected the emphasis, urgency, and the gravity of this request.[2] It's no small "Mickey Mouse" prayer. It's gutsy, unapologetic, unashamed, passionate, and charged with expectancy. It's a prayer that shouts, "God can and God will!" It makes you wonder if Jabez knew something elusive about God that most people aren't acquainted with. Perhaps he was fully persuaded that God is a lavish Father who is always ready to bless unconditionally, without reservation, without hesitation.

We hear the word *bless* or *blessing* in many different settings—during the benediction at a church service, when praying over our food, even when someone sneezes. That the meaning of blessing has been relegated to something bland and hollow like "see you later" is no wonder. In the biblical sense, "to bless" means to impart supernatural favor. When we entreat God's blessing, we are asking for His power, His infinite goodness and benevolence, His unmerited favor that we cannot earn in our own capacity, that only He can lavish on us. *"The Lord's blessing is our greatest wealth. All our work adds nothing to it"* (Proverbs 10:22 TLB).

> **WHEN WE ENTREAT GOD'S BLESSING, WE ARE ASKING FOR HIS POWER, HIS INFINITE GOODNESS AND BENEVOLENCE, HIS UNMERITED FAVOR THAT WE CANNOT EARN IN OUR OWN CAPACITY, THAT ONLY HE CAN LAVISH ON US.**

King David reminds us of God's propensity to bless and provide for His people:

> *How great is the goodness you have stored up for those who fear you. You lavish it on those who come to you for protection, blessing them before the watching world.* (Psalm 31:19 NLT)

The Hebrew word for *"great"* in this verse means abundant, many, large in number, mighty, exceedingly, multiply, and princely.[3] I think it is safe to say that God's goodness is over the top! David must have well understood the heart of the Father, who loves to lavish His goodness on His children. And, by the way, the world gets to witness Him love on His children and show them off. What a Dad!

"MY NAME IS JIMMY—GIMME, GIMME, GIMME!"

You may say, "Wait a minute, Jabez's prayer sounds narcissistic and self-indulgent. I don't think we are to approach God as if He's some sort of genie in a bottle, or a cosmic slot machine, demanding

Him to bow down to our whims and fancies." You are right. I agree with you. Are we to treat Jabez's prayer like a formula for coveting personal blessing? Absolutely not. First, nothing in the traditions of Judaism and Christianity discourages believers from seeking blessing from God. So, that's not the issue. The danger is when we abuse the truth. This is not magical incantation—it's not as if we mutter a request and God responds on demand.

The ability to bless is the divine prerogative of God. We don't dictate how God operates. After all, He is God. I am not advocating a "My name is Jimmy—gimme, gimme, gimme" self-centered gospel devoid of kingdom responsibility. Praying boldly for God's blessings does not annul our responsibility to live with contentment, taking care of the poor and needy, preferring others above ourselves, wisely stewarding His resources and blessings—all principles that the Bible clearly teaches. Balance is the key.

On the other hand, I'm not drawn to a gospel that strips God's children from the freedom to enjoy His blessings. God is God all by Himself. A magnanimous, all-knowing, and all-wise Father, He knows when, where, how, and the extent to which to bless His children. Our job is to ask in agreement with His will, always honoring Him for who He is, beyond what He can do for us.

> *You do not have because you do not ask. You ask and do not receive, because you ask with wrong motives, so that you may spend it on your pleasures.*   (James 4:2–3 NASB)

When we ask and do not receive, it does not mean that God is a killjoy or a party pooper. It does not take away His propensity to bless. He is still God. James shows us that we don't receive because we ask with the wrong motives—to indulge in pleasures that are at war within our souls. God wants to give us good gifts. He wants us to enjoy His blessings. However, He is not quick to answer self-gratifying prayers that do not honor God or others. When Jesus promised us, *"Ask, and it will be given to you"* (Matthew 7:7), He was referring to asking that is centered on God's name,

His kingdom, and His will. Ultimately, we have to trust that God knows what is the best for us and what best serves His purposes.

> GOD WANTS TO GIVE US GOOD GIFTS. HE WANTS US TO ENJOY HIS BLESSINGS. HOWEVER, HE IS NOT QUICK TO ANSWER SELF-GRATIFYING PRAYERS THAT DO NOT HONOR GOD OR OTHERS.

HARD TIME RECEIVING

"Cornelius, if you don't learn how to receive, you will never be blessed," Joseph said to me.

A generous individual had bought an expensive ticket to the Broadway musical *Joseph and the Amazing Technicolor Dreamcoat* and wanted to bless me with it. The person wished to remain anonymous and have Joseph give the ticket to me. I had never been to a professional musical before, and I had always desired to go. I was thrilled by the opportunity, but I felt so undeserving of the gift.

I said to Joe, "This is too much. I don't deserve such an expensive gift. Please return the gift."

I don't know how this self-deprecation developed in my life and thoughts. Perhaps it is because, in Asian culture, I was brought up with the mentality that nothing comes free. We are an industrious, hardworking people. Unless you are born with a silver spoon in your mouth, you have to work really hard to earn a good living. Perhaps some of you can relate to that. Herein lies my issue—unhealthy striving. This is how it translated and played out in most of my Christian life. I always felt that I had to work really hard to earn God's approval and blessings. I had no understanding of the unconditional concept of grace. My unhealthy striving proved to be the very antithesis of grace. I had to pray more, read the Bible more, sacrifice more, fast more, have more faith, confess His Word more...the duties go on and on. I believed I had to work up my spirituality for God to bless me.

When we don't understand God's free-giving grace, we end up repelling His blessings.

NOT WORTHY?

The struggle for most people is not whether God is able to bless; they believe in that. The issue is that many don't feel like they are worthy of His blessings. Perhaps like Jabez, you tell yourself, "I am not educated enough." "I am not good looking enough." "I always make the wrong decisions. " "I am a single mom." "I am divorced." "I have the wrong skin color." "My life is nothing but pain. " "Surely God's blessings are for someone else." "I'm just not worthy." I think Jabez would have an encouraging word for you today:

> I've been there. I was born in pain. My name is pain. My life didn't look like it was worthy of any good. I didn't feel like I deserved anything. But it didn't stopped me from lifting my eyes above my circumstances and praying to God with audacious faith to bless me indeed! I know without a doubt that He is good and He is no respecter of persons. He will be good to you too!

The blessings of God are free gifts of His grace and love for us. They are bestowed on us not because of how good we are but how good He is. God's nature is to bless. It's who He is. He can't default Himself. He is that good!

"Cornelius, if you don't learn how to receive, you will never be blessed." Those words set me on a journey of freedom from false humility, and gave me the confidence to receive God's blessings freely, without guilt and striving.

Quit doubting and limiting His goodness, and start believing and embracing His lavish heart toward you. Right believing will lead to right receiving. I love how the writer of *The Message* puts it succinctly:

> *Don't bargain with God. Be direct. Ask for what you need. This isn't a cat-and-mouse, hide-and-seek game we're in. If your child asks for bread, do you trick him with sawdust? If he asks for fish,*

*do you scare him with a live snake on his plate? As bad as you
are, you wouldn't think of such a thing. You're at least decent to
your own children. So don't you think the God who conceived
you in love will be even better?*   (Matthew 7:1–11 MSG)

"OH, THAT YOUR HAND WOULD BE WITH ME!"

As mentioned before, "hand of the Lord" (see 1 Chronicles
4:10) is a biblical reference to God's power and provision in our lives.
Jabez knew that he needed to depend on the hand of the Lord to
work mightily on his behalf. Jabez knew that, for his destiny to turn
around, he desperately needed God's hand to intervene. And God
granted his request.

Jabez understood that the place of dependence is the place of
humility and trust. Dependence on God demands our surrender.
Our surrendered lives will become the foundation on which His
unlimited opportunities will flourish. Asking for God's hand to be
upon our lives activates and releases His presence, power, and provision. Let me share with you a simple story to bring home the message.

> WHEN THE LORD'S STRONG HAND IS UPON OUR LIVES,
> OUR PERSPECTIVE CHANGES.
> WE BEGIN TO SEE OUR LIVES AND NEEDS AS HE SEES THEM.

A father leads his two-year-old girl by her little pinkie into an elevator at a shopping mall. Without a care in the world, she stares out
the glass windows, intrigued by the view and ready to experience the
thrill of gravity. Soon, more people start entering the elevator, and it
gets congested. Surrounded by towering individuals on all sides, the
little girl begins to panic. She cries out, "Daddy, Daddy, pick me up!
Pick me up!" shooting both arms up toward her dad.

The dad stoops down, extends his arms, and pulls her up tight
to his chest, her head now inches above her neighbors. When she is
elevated and in the safety of her dad's arms, a beautiful smile returns

to her countenance. She hears her dad say, "Honey, you're fine. It's okay. I've got you."

When the Lord's strong hand is upon our lives, our perspective changes. We begin to see our lives and needs as He sees them. He lifts us up from our lack. He elevates our faith. We begin to experience His provision at another level.

"Oh, that Your hand would be with me!"

PRAYER OF FAITH

At every place where I have shared this message, I have asked the people to do a prophetic act. Stretch out your right hand toward heaven. I want you to imagine the Lord's right hand reaching down and clasping yours as He releases His power and provision for all your needs. Pray this with me:

> Father, I pray that You would bless me indeed, and enlarge my territory, that Your hand would be with me, and that You would keep me from evil. I thank You that I receive from Your right hand of authority, power, and provision. I thank You and praise You in advance for all the breakthroughs and miracles that You are performing on my behalf. In Your most powerful name, I pray, amen!

3

SO, REALLY, WHO IS THE LORD?

"If we command our wealth, we shall be rich and free; if our
wealth commands us, we are poor indeed."[1]
—Edmund Burke

People often ask me, "Cornelius, we love the stories and testimonies about God's provision in your life. What is the key to experiencing divine provision?" Inevitably, my answer is, "Lordship." Christ's disciples are called to the high standard of single-hearted devotion. We face many everyday concerns that can deter us from prioritizing God's kingdom and its righteousness. At the heart of the matter is the matter of the heart. This chapter focuses on three teachings of Jesus in Matthew 6—"*treasures*" (verse 19), "*the eye*" (verse 22), and "*masters*" (verse 24)—that warned against the idolatrous seduction of wealth and possessions. Put on your student hat, and let's learn from Rabbi Jesus.

Material wealth was desired by Jews because it was indicative of God's blessing. At the same time, the people of Israel knew that a person's spirituality and final standing before God was not ultimately measured by a person's wealth.[2] Wealth in and of itself is neutral. However, it can be deceptive, and the accumulation of it for selfish means can lead to all kinds of evils. It can provide a false sense of security and a fallacious assessment of one's spirituality.

TEACHING 1: WHAT'S IN YOUR STORAGE?

> *Do not lay up for yourselves treasures on earth, where moth and rust destroy and where thieves break in and steal; but lay up for yourselves treasures in heaven, where neither moth nor rust destroys and where thieves do not break in and steal.*
>
> (Matthew 6:19–20)

Jesus begins by giving a negative imperative: *"Do not lay up"* treasures or valuables on earth that have a short life span. *"Where moth and rust destroy and where thieves break in and steal"* highlights the truth that treasures stored up on earth will not endure, where they are subjected to the destructive effects of nature and a fallen world. In the ancient world, two things were considered part of a person's treasures—cloth and metal. Thus, owners of these valuables were worried about moth and rust, which were typical in Palestine. The moth was notorious for destroying clothing, and was often used to symbolize destruction. (See Isaiah 50:9, 51:8; Job 4:19.) Similarly, rust destroys a variety of materials, such as metal, crops, vines, and even teeth.[3] Houses were made of mud bricks or baked clay, and treasures were often buried underground. Thieves could easily dig and steal valued possessions. Evidently, moth, rust, and thieves could depreciate and destroy earthly possessions.

Elsewhere, Jesus taught a parable about the dangers of materialism. The fool in the parable, who *"lays up treasure for himself, and is not rich toward God"* (Luke 12:21), fails to understand one of life's lessons, that his possessions are gifts to be used unselfishly in accordance with God's will and are not to be hoarded.

THE RICH YOUNG RULER

In a complementary teaching about the lure of riches, the rich young ruler asked Jesus what he must do to get saved. Jesus replied,

> *One thing you lack: Go your way, sell whatever you have and give to the poor, and you will have treasure in heaven; and come, take up the cross, and follow Me.* (Mark 10:21)

The Bible says that the young man went away sorrowful because he had great possessions. (See Mark 10:22.) Jesus then directed His attention to the disciples and made a stunning remark: *"How hard it is for those who have riches to enter the kingdom of God!"* (Mark 10:23). He emphasized, *"Children, how hard it is for those who trust in riches to enter the kingdom of God!"* (Mark 10:24) Then Jesus dropped a bombshell on them: *"It is easier for a camel to go through the eye of a needle than for a rich man to enter the kingdom of God"* (Mark 10:25). The Jews saw wealth as a mark of God's favor, so it would have been inconceivable that riches would be an impediment to kingdom life. One could almost imagine the shock of the disciples, their mouths gaping as they heard these words. Jesus reveals the fallacy of such a view, and resorts to vivid hyperbole to reinforce that he who puts his trust in wealth and possessions will not enter heaven.

Mark intentionally highlighted the heart of the Father in this passage. The second time Jesus spoke to the disciples about this topic, He addressed them as *"children"* (Mark 10:24)—the first and only time in the gospel. I believe Jesus would have said these words to reassure them: "My children, I know this is a tall order, but look to your heavenly Father. Trust me. He's got your back."

Moments before, Jesus had chided the disciples for not welcoming the little children.

> But when Jesus saw it, He was greatly displeased and said to them, "Let the little children come to Me, and do not forbid them; for of such is the kingdom of God. Assuredly, I say to you, whoever does not receive the kingdom of God as a little child will by no means enter it."   (Mark 10:14–15)

Jesus referred to a child's innocence, trusting heart, and dependence on his or her parents to assert that the kingdom of God is reserved for those who choose not to put their trust in riches but who choose to be vulnerable, trusting their heavenly Father for their needs.

Soon after, Jesus reassured the disciples that the rewards of God would far outweigh their sacrifice. In Mark 10:29, He mentioned leaving one's earthly family members to follow Him and, interestingly, "fathers" were excluded in the relationships Jesus said the disciples would inherit in the kingdom. (See Mark 10:30.) This omission suggests that Jesus wanted His disciples to know God alone is their Father, their Provider.[4]

> *So Jesus answered and said, "Assuredly, I say to you, there is no one who has left house or brothers or sisters or father or mother or wife or children or lands, for My sake and the gospel's, who shall not receive a hundredfold now in this time—houses and brothers and sisters and mothers and children and lands, with persecutions—and in the age to come, eternal life.*
>
> (Mark 10:29–30)

In the ancient world, the command to sell everything would have sounded like good advice to those who were spiritually devout. However, you don't need to sell your home, empty your bank account, and check yourself into a monastery to enter the kingdom of God. That is not the point. God is not opposed to us having wealth and possessions; the point is not to let these things master us. To enter the kingdom of God, we must submit to God's rule so that He has lordship over all aspects of our lives. The rich young ruler could not bring himself to let go of his material possessions—not even for eternal life. If he had let those things go, Jesus may have allowed him to keep them. Jesus's radical demands may be a tough pill to swallow for many in our materialistic society, but His love is jealous for us, and He will not settle for divided allegiance.

GOD IS NOT OPPOSED TO US HAVING WEALTH AND POSSESSIONS; THE POINT IS NOT TO LET THESE THINGS MASTER US. TO ENTER THE KINGDOM OF GOD, WE MUST SUBMIT TO GOD'S RULE SO THAT HE HAS LORDSHIP OVER ALL ASPECTS OF OUR LIVES.

It is important to mention that Jesus does not look at the rich any differently than the poor. Jesus does not look down on the wealthy as second-class if they struggle with kingdom priorities. The rich young ruler turned his back on Jesus, but Jesus did not turn His back on him. In fact, before Jesus told him to go sell all his possessions and follow Him, Jesus looked at him and *"loved him"* (Mark 10:21). Jesus did not soften His demands for total allegiance; neither did He love the young man any less.

In response to Jesus's call for radical discipleship, Peter exclaimed, *"We have left all and followed You"* (Mark 10:28). Jesus is no debtor to anyone, but He is detailed and magnanimous in His rewards. Jesus's high demands for sacrificial discipleship are met with the promise of His provision and blessings. Those who have left everything for the sake of the gospel, albeit *"with persecutions,"* will receive a *"hundred-fold"* reward in this lifetime and eternal life in the age to come (Mark 10:30). The disciples were itinerant preachers, and their giving up of family and land does not refer to a total severance of family ties but to leaving family and possessions for a period when they were doing ministry on the road.[5] Also, a recompense of a *"hundredfold"* (verse 30) did not mean a prosperity bumper but the blessings they would receive from the community of faith, the family of the followers of Christ everywhere the disciples went.[6] It was not a spiritual ticket to get rich, as some would believe. The anticlimactic sting at the end of this list of blessings is Mark's mention of *"persecutions"* (verse 30), suggesting that Mark was not validating a prosperity gospel. It serves to remind the disciples and the modern believer that, although the Christian faith does not exempt them from hardships and adversity, the loving heavenly Father cares and He will provide.

TREASURES IN HEAVEN

So instead of storing up earthly valuables that don't last, we are to *"store up for yourselves treasures in heaven"* (Matthew 6:20 NIV). Jesus does not define what these treasures are, but the Jews would have been very accustomed to this concept and practice of storing up good works before God, such as the generous act of providing for someone in need.[7]

In Matthew 6, Jesus taught about various acts of righteousness, like prayer, fasting, and almsgiving. (See Matthew 6:1–18.) These and other God-honoring deeds the disciples regularly practiced fit into the description of *"treasures in heaven."*

In the New Testament, the apostle Paul teaches extensively about "seeking and setting the mind on things that are above" (see Colossians 3:1) and about the judgment of every believer's work for the kingdom on judgment day (see 1 Corinthians 3:12–15). It is clear that treasures in heaven are stored up by obedience to God's commands and seeking His will in all areas of our lives.

JESUS IS NOT AGAINST WEALTH

Although wealth is a potential danger to faith, Jesus never categorically condemned it. Joseph of Arimathea (see Mark 15:43) and Mary of Bethany (see John 12:3), among others, were never reprimanded for being wealthy. Many of us have cringed at the thought of ministers manipulating the Bible to fatten their bank accounts at the expense of well-meaning believers. Although I am not a proponent of a wealth gospel, I am a firm advocate of prosperity with a purpose. Prosperity isn't necessarily bad. It is not an end in itself; it serves as a means to an end in the kingdom of God.

> PROSPERITY ISN'T NECESSARILY BAD. IT IS NOT AN END IN ITSELF;
> IT SERVES AS A MEANS TO AN END IN THE KINGDOM OF GOD.

The pursuit of wealth or anything without a kingdom purpose attached to it is, at best, self-serving, giving temporary pleasure, and, at worst, idolatry. Jesus did not eliminate the desire for wealth; He simply redirected it—to a greater purpose and higher priority that demands wise stewardship of resources. Most religions' are ascetic in nature, advising their adherents to eschew human ambition, success, and wealth. Jesus, however, teaches us to elevate our ambition and wealth for His cause—to meet the needs of His people and to expand His glorious kingdom. Money is not the root of all evil; the insatiable appetite for it is.

For the love of money is a root of all kinds of evil, for which some have strayed from the faith in their greediness, and pierced themselves through with many sorrows. But you, O man of God, flee these things and pursue righteousness, godliness, faith, love, patience, gentleness. Fight the good fight of faith, lay hold on eternal life, to which you were also called and have confessed the good confession in the presence of many witnesses.

(1 Timothy 6:10–12)

Jesus's differentiation of treasures on earth and treasures in heaven points out a sharp contrast of values. (See Matthew 6:19–20.) As Christ followers, if we value what God values above what society values, we will live in a spirit of generosity, not hoarding wealth and possessions but intentionally looking for opportunities to bless others in need.

Many of Jesus's disciples weren't wealthy; neither were many of the peasants, farmers, and tradesmen who came to listen to Jesus. His warning about wealth and possessions wasn't directed just to wealthy people. The lure of wealth is a universal issue; even those with little are warned about its dangers. Jesus's teaching here may bother modern hearers, those who are accustomed to always having excess. It is tempting to explain away Jesus's radical teachings regarding wealth rather than to find relevant applications for them. If we as Christ followers fully trust God, we will prioritize treasures in heaven.

THE HEART REVEALS

For where your treasure is, there your heart will be also.

(Matthew 6:21)

A treasure refers to what one prizes most in his heart. Jesus had taught that good or bad deeds are first committed in the heart. (See Matthew 5:28.) The heart represents the core of a person's being; it affects the whole person, spiritually, emotionally, and psychologically. The choices a person makes, for God or self, reveal the values of his heart and, more significantly, his spiritual priorities. Billy Graham said, "Give me five minutes with a person's checkbook, and I will tell you where their heart is."[8]

> The heart is deceitful above all things, and desperately wicked; who can know it? (Jeremiah 17:9)

I have met many people who have expressed their desire to honor God with their wealth and possessions, only to get trapped in the mire of greed and selfish ambition. They invest their time, energy, and life in accumulating treasures that will eventually rot and fail. Jesus said that all our hearts will be revealed. "*A tree is known by its fruit*" (Matthew 12:33), "*Every good tree bears good fruit, and a bad tree bears bad fruit*" (Matthew 7:17).

TEACHING 2: "I WANT A GOOD EYE!"

Sandwiched between two passages teaching about wealth and possessions is a passage talking about the eye, a subject seemingly random and out of place. This enigmatic passage must be understood in light of the preceding and subsequent passages. Jesus switches to a different metaphor here, but the message remains the same—His standard for the disciples' perspective and application concerning possessions. It is a call for undistracted loyalty to God.

> The lamp of the body is the eye. If therefore your eye is good, your whole body will be full of light. But if your eye is bad, your whole body will be full of darkness. If therefore the light that is in you is darkness, how great is that darkness! (Matthew 6:22–23)

Jesus continues the theme of treasure by explaining that the eye is a lamp that illumines the inner life of a person. In ancient writings, the eye was understood to be a window through which light enters the body, suggesting that light is important to the inside of a body. The lamp metaphor may more naturally reflect the function of the eye in providing light to the body to find its way.[9] For the body to work well, the eye must be healthy. In this sense, we might expect a "good" eye to be healthy and a "bad" eye to be diseased. However, the Greek word for "*good*" used in this passage is *haplous*, which literally means "single."[10] This suggests that there is more to what makes an eye good or healthy. There's more to what meets the eye. An obvious implication would be single-mindedness or undistracted sight, adding weight to what Jesus had already emphasized about spiritual priorities in Matthew 6:19–21, as well as the forthcoming incisive charge in verse 24—one cannot serve both God and mammon.

The "single eye" metaphor is used to describe a life that is wholeheartedly devoted to God and His kingdom purposes. Another probable use of the word *haplous* is to indicate generosity, which is made clear when contrasted with the bad (*ponēros*) eye, a Semitic metaphor meaning stinginess, greed, and jealousy.[11] Given this, people's spiritual health can be reflected in their generosity or lack of it, in how they steward their material possessions.

> *He who has a generous eye will be blessed, for he gives of his bread to the poor.*   (Proverbs 22:9)

The dual usage of the word *haplous* shows an intentional double entendre, elucidating not only the theme of undistracted loyalty but generosity. A good eye will lead to a well-illuminated body. The lamp or the eye provides light for the body to find its way; a life in the light is the fruit of a life lived solely for God's purposes. On the other hand, a life in darkness is the fruit of a bad eye, motivated by selfish materialism and blinded to the ways and priorities of kingdom living.

TEACHING 3: CHOOSE ONE

> *No one can serve two masters; for either he will hate the one and love the other, or else he will be loyal to the one and despise the other. You cannot serve God and mammon.*   (Matthew 6:24)

Jesus taught about the two treasures (earth and heaven), two eyes (good and bad), and, now, two masters (God and mammon). For the Christ follower, there is no cutting corners, no double dipping. Jesus applies this principle to one of the greatest temptations: the idolatry of materialism. The passages on the treasures and the eyes call for single-minded devotion and loyalty to God, and verse 24 warns of the double-mindedness that leads to spiritual idolatry.

Mammon is an Aramaic word that means "wealth" and "property."[12] Modern versions translate it as "money," "gold," or "material possessions."[13] It is likely a derivative from a root word that means "that in which one trust[s]."[14] Although the word itself is neutral, its common usage was derogatory. Mammon was used to describe dishonest profits gained from the exploitation of others, synonymous with what Jesus called *"unrighteous mammon"* (Luke 16:9).[15]

Slavery was common in ancient times, and slaves had to be completely devoted to a single owner. Jesus's original audience would have been cognizant of its implications. In Jewish culture, the worship of money functioned as a *reductio ad absurdum*; the consequences of such idolatry were absurd.[16] In other words, it is ludicrous to put your trust in money. It's plain stupidity. In fact, even the Gentiles would ridicule a person who worshiped money.

The early Christians understood that a person could gain the world and forfeit his or her soul. Serving two masters is congruous with these words of Jesus:

> *For what profit is it to a man if he gains the whole world, and loses his own soul? Or what will a man give in exchange for his soul? For the Son of Man will come in the glory of His Father with His angels, and then He will reward each according to his works.*   (Matthew 16:26–27)

Materialism and covetousness are pervasive in our culture. It's percolated through the church such that the radical words of Jesus, and the call to sole allegiance to Him, have become more of a peripheral idea than a mandate for most Christians.

MAMMON IS A SPIRITUAL FORCE SO ATTRACTIVE THAT IT LURES MANY INTO ITS EVIL TRAPPINGS AND DISQUALIFIES BELIEVERS FROM FAITHFUL AND EFFECTIVE SERVICE FOR CHRIST.

Jesus clearly presents an ultimatum between choosing God or mammon so that we can't rationalize it away. It applies to every believer today, not just to the spiritually zealous. Mammon is a spiritual force so attractive that it lures many into its evil trappings and disqualifies believers from faithful and effective service for Christ. Spiritually, it is a stronghold that needs to be broken in people's lives. Practically, in our daily decisions, I believe we can loosen its hold on us by intentionally moving in the spirit of generosity and sacrifice.

> *Command those who are rich in this present age not to be haughty, nor to trust in uncertain riches but in the living God, who gives us richly all things to enjoy. Let them do good, that they be rich in good works, ready to give, willing to share, storing up for themselves a good foundation for the time to come, that they may lay hold on eternal life.* (1 Timothy 6:17–19)

The central thrust of this series of teachings (treasure, eye, masters) in Matthew 6 is an undistracted and unadulterated commitment to God and His kingdom purposes. Wealth easily distracts people from true discipleship. A disciple's attitude toward money and material possessions often reveals the depth of his commitment to God. It shows his heart's priorities and affections. There is no need to suppose that Jesus is advocating an ascetic lifestyle that denies the people of God the good things in life. However, we must be sensitive enough to discern when wealth and possessions subtly divert us away from true discipleship.

> *If riches increase, do not set your heart on them.* (Psalm 62:10)

PRAYER OF FAITH

God is our loving Father, and His love is jealous. He is after our hearts and undivided devotion. Invite the Holy Spirit to show you what has become an idol in your life, whether it's wealth and riches or material possessions. As you repent and renounce their hold and reset the primacy of God over your life, position yourself to receive from the Father, your sole Provider. Make the following declarations:

- Father, I choose You, above all else, as my Lord.
- I choose to be single-minded; my eyes are set on You.
- I choose You over mammon.
- I choose to seek the kingdom first as my priority.
- I choose to store up treasures in heaven rather than be consumed by treasures on earth.
- I choose to put my trust in You and Your ability to provide.
- I renounce the power of greed.
- I renounce the idolatry of materialism.
- I renounce worry and anxiety.
- I renounce the lie that wealth is evil.
- I renounce the lie that You cannot meet all my needs.
- I renounce the lie that I can never have more than enough.
- I bless my spirit to be full of faith.
- I bless my spirit to be generous.
- I bless my spirit to receive abundance and all that You have for me.
- I declare that You will supply all my needs according to Your riches in glory.

Now, go ahead and thank the Lord!

4

WORRY—YOUR WORST INVESTMENT

"Worry is a practical atheism and an affront to God."[1]
—Robert Mounce

Two business executives met for lunch. Gene asked Ed, "How's your health?"

Ed said, "I feel great! My ulcers are gone, and I don't have a care in the world!"

Gene asked, "How did that happen?"

Ed replied, "Well, you know my doctor told me my ulcers were caused by worrying. So, I hired a professional worrier. When something worrisome comes up, I turn it over to him, and he does all my worrying for me!"

"Wow, I'd like to hire someone like that! How much does he charge?"

"One hundred thousand dollars!" Ed replied.

Gene retorted, "How in the world can you afford one hundred thousand dollars?"

Ed said, "I don't know. I let him worry about that!"

Don't we all wish we can subcontract all the worrying, stressing, and "anxietying" to someone else? Worry is like mosquitoes—they come around from time to time, and they serve no purpose but to suck your blood! We all know what worrying feels like. Jesus addresses the issue of worry and exhorts us to trust in our heavenly Father's providential care. (See Matthew 6:25–34.) Worry is the antithesis of faith in God. The Greek meaning of the words *"Do not worry"* (Matthew 6:25) is emphatic in nature; it is not a suggestion from Jesus.[2] The exhortation to not worry is mentioned three times in this passage alone. Jesus told His disciples that worry is pointless and futile. Someone once said that worrying is like a rocking chair: it gives you something to do, but gets you nowhere. It is one of the worst investments you can make in your life. It yields zero profit every single time.

More than likely, Jesus's audience came from poorer backgrounds. Food, drink, clothing, and the basic necessities may have been a cause of anxiety to most. Ironically, in America and other affluent nations, where we have access to more than the basic necessities, we haven't fared much better. Jesus asked a rhetorical question to make a point—namely, that existence (life and the body) is more than food and clothing, as necessary and essential as they are.

> *Therefore I say to you, do not worry about your life, what you will eat or what you will drink; nor about your body, what you will put on. Is not life more than food and the body more than clothing?* (Matthew 6:25)

He wanted His disciples to understand that if He is the Source of life and the body, then He is more than able to provide for needs like food and clothing.

> *Look at the birds of the air, for they neither sow nor reap nor gather into barns; yet your heavenly Father feeds them. Are you not of more value than they? Which of you by worrying can add one cubit to his stature? So why do you worry about clothing? Consider the lilies of the field, how they grow: they neither toil nor spin; and yet I say to you that even Solomon in all his glory was not arrayed like one of these. Now if God so clothes the grass of the field, which today is, and tomorrow is thrown into the*

oven, will He not much more clothe you, O you of little faith?
(Matthew 6:26–30)

Jesus twice used a traditional Jewish argument—*qal wahomer,* which starts with a lesser point that supports a greater point—to emphasize that He would care for them.[3] If God takes care of the birds of the air and the flowers of the fields, which cannot provide for themselves, how much more will He, the loving Father, take care of His beloved children who are created in His image? Jesus never condemned His disciples for recognizing their basic needs for food and clothing; He knew that they needed them. Yet He called them to depend on Him for their daily sustenance.

In Jewish culture, it was absurd to put one's trust in wealth and material possessions. It was also considered absurd to be anxious. Jews also know that God provides for the birds of the air and the fish of the sea. Birds in the wild are tirelessly industrious; the sparrow is one of the busiest creatures of nature. Jesus was not discouraging hard work to provide for our needs; neither was He asking us to strive and be as busy as the sparrows. Jesus's rhetorical question *"Are you not of more value than they?"* (Matthew 6:26) reveals that if the disciples were worth more than the birds, then they could be assured of God's providential care for their needs, just as the birds depend on God for theirs.

To add weight to what He just said, Jesus followed up with another rhetorical question, *"Which of you by worrying can add one cubit to his stature?"* (Matthew 6:27). In this context, *"stature"* means "length of time," and *"cubit"* means "a fraction of time."[4] Jesus was accentuating that worrying is of no use; you cannot extend your life by even a small fraction of time by being anxious! Winston Churchill, the great prime minister of the United Kingdom, once said, "When I look back on all these worries I remember the story of the old man who said on his deathbed that he had a lot of trouble in his life, most of which had never happened."[5]

So why do you worry about clothing? Consider the lilies of the field, how they grow: they neither toil nor spin; and yet I say to

*you that even Solomon in all his glory was not arrayed like one of
these. Now if God so clothes the grass of the field, which today is,
and tomorrow is thrown into the oven, will He not much more
clothe you, O you of little faith?*   (Matthew 6:28–30)

Jesus switched metaphors and used the flower to address the
foolishness of anxiety for clothing. Here, Jesus used the words *"how
they grow: they neither toil nor spin"* to highlight that flowers do not
twist layers of yarn together to make thread—labor that is necessary
to make clothes. And yet they are clothed in beauty and glory that
surpasses the riches of Solomon!

In ancient times in the Middle East, the grass was used to fuel the
oven. It is still used this way today. The implication here is obvious:
If God so wonderfully clothes what is evanescent and valueless, how
much more will He provide clothing for the disciples? Again, Jesus
did not use this illustration to suggest indolence or passivity. He used
yet again a qal wahomer—*"will He not much more clothe you…?"*—to
emphasize God's care for His children.

MY FAVORITE SHIRTS

Years ago, as a teenager growing up in Singapore, I would work
just so I could shop. Singapore is a paradise for shopping. It is a very
modern, affluent, and trendy city. There, shopping is a national pas-
time, next to eating. Sounds like a glorious place, doesn't it? You all
should visit.

Except, there was a slight problem. I was a compulsive shop-
per. Spending money on clothes wasn't just to meet a basic need so I
didn't walk around naked. It was chick magnet tactic number one, my
occasionally effective but downright pathetic attempt to impress the
ladies. Don't judge. When I started learning about kingdom priorities
and stewarding my resources well, one of the lifestyle adjustments I
had to make was cutting down my spending on clothing. Sometimes,
I had to deliberately avoid the shopping malls as if they were a plague
because they are everywhere in Singapore!

At that time, I really liked these fancy, guaranteed-to-score-a-date, pricey shirts from a particular store. I couldn't afford them. One day, a friend who had no idea about my taste and appreciation for those shirts came up to me with a shopping bag of clothes. Guess what was inside? Five brand-new, crisp shirts from that store. This is more than about being Mr. Swaggalicious or impressing the ladies. It's about the Father's meticulous attention to details. If He can send a bunch of birds to bring bread and meat to Elijah morning and evening, you can trust that, in His out-of-the-box creativity and illimitable capacity, He will provide for you.

Jesus scolded His disciples, calling them *"you of little faith"* (Matthew 8:26), implying that they fell short of the appropriate level of faith and confidence in God's ability to provide for them. Matthew used the term *"little faith"* elsewhere, revealing the disciples' lack of trust in situations of physical need. (See Matthew 14:31, 16:8.)

Before Jesus taught the disciples the Lord's Prayer, He assured them, *"Your Father knows the things you have need of before you ask Him"* (Matthew 6:8). And He said, *"For your heavenly Father knows that you need all these things"* (Matthew 6:32). In Jewish writing, when something is repeated, it is for the sake of emphasis. He knows your needs! He really knows your needs!

DILIGENCE IS GOOD

Jesus's forbiddance of worry does not suggest that we should ignore our concerns or deny their existence. It also does not call into question a person's responsibility to provide for his own needs or family. It does not imply that food, drink, clothing, and other basic necessities will come automatically without work and diligent planning for the future. The virtues of diligence and hard work are prominent themes in the book of Proverbs. Jesus's concern, consistent with what we have already established, involves our priorities. We are called to have unrivaled discipleship and undistracted loyalty to God, His kingdom, and His righteousness. Jesus is opposed to paralyzing anxiety that weakens our commitment to discipleship.

> **WE ARE CALLED TO HAVE UNRIVALED DISCIPLESHIP AND UNDISTRACTED LOYALTY TO GOD, HIS KINGDOM, AND HIS RIGHTEOUSNESS. JESUS IS OPPOSED TO PARALYZING ANXIETY THAT WEAKENS OUR COMMITMENT TO DISCIPLESHIP.**

In addition, Jesus does not leave us to fend for ourselves. He expects us to express our utter dependence on him for all our concerns and needs, praying for and requesting them. He taught us to pray, *"Give us this day our daily bread"* (Matthew 6:11). We are taught to pray and ask with the motivation *"Your kingdom come. Your will be done"* (Matthew 6:10), a kingdom priority.

> *Therefore do not worry, saying, "What shall we eat?" or "What shall we drink?" or "What shall we wear?" For after all these things the Gentiles seek. For your heavenly Father knows that you need all these things. But seek first the kingdom of God and His righteousness, and all these things shall be added to you. Therefore do not worry about tomorrow, for tomorrow will worry about its own things. Sufficient for the day is its own trouble.* (Matthew 6:31–34)

By faith, God's children have access to the providential care of the Father, who *"knows that you need all these things"* (verse 32). The word *"seek"* (verse 33) is in the present imperative tense in Greek, indicating an ongoing obligation to God's kingdom and His righteousness.[6] The Christ follower should be wholeheartedly committed to learn, discover, and, ultimately, fulfill the will of God in all areas of his life. When we prioritize His will and His kingdom purposes above our material concerns, He promises that *"all these things"* (verse 32)—the fullness of God's provision—will be added to us. Frederick Bruner, a famous theologian, could not have said it better:

> While disciples are seeking God's kingdom in the front room of their lives, possessions will be brought around to the back door and deposited in the kitchen. The Father has a

delivery service that brings those things for which the world spends its whole time shopping.[7]

Trusting God for our material needs does not mean we will have a smooth-sailing life without challenges. But while the worldly people are consumed with anxiety over their needs, God's people have the power of faith in the heavenly Father. The essence of faith is not the denial of reality; it is trusting in a heavenly power who can affect and transform our immediate circumstances. Matthew closes this passage by encouraging us to not burden ourselves with tomorrow's troubles by worrying. God's sovereign care and His loving nature guarantee that they will be taken care of when the time comes. We can count on God's faithfulness on a daily basis.

> Come now, you who say, "Today or tomorrow we will go to such and such a city, spend a year there, buy and sell, and make a profit"; whereas you do not know what will happen tomorrow. For what is your life? It is even a vapor that appears for a little time and then vanishes away. Instead, you ought to say, "If the Lord wills, we shall live and do this or that." (James 4:13–15)

The first disciples were full-time itinerant preachers. Most of us hold jobs in the marketplace, and have various financial commitments (for example, a mortgage, car, credit card payments, college loans, insurance, and so forth). Although we live in a different era, setting, culture, and lifestyle than the disciples, we are still charged to put our faith and trust in God for all our needs. This passage is just as relevant to us today as it was for the early disciples. Worry and anxiety are incompatible with the lifestyle of the believer whose priority is set on God and His kingdom purposes. Jesus is after our heart's devotion. Are our hearts consumed with wealth and riches, worry and anxiety? The heart is the control center that directs everything that concerns our lives.

> Keep your heart with all diligence, for out of it spring the issues of life.   (Proverbs 4:23)

Let me close with a story from the thirteenth-century German mystic Johann Tauler.

> One day Tauler met a beggar.
>
> "God give you a good day, my friend," he said.
>
> The beggar answered, "I thank God I never had a bad one."
>
> Then Tauler said, "God give you a happy life, my friend."
>
> "I thank God," said the beggar, "that I am never unhappy."
>
> In amazement Tauler asked, "What do you mean?"
>
> "Well," said the beggar, "When it is fine I thank God. When it rains I thank God. When I have plenty I thank God. When I am hungry I thank God. And, since God's will is my will, and whatever pleases him pleases me, why should I say I am unhappy when I am not?"
>
> Tauler looked at the man in astonishment. "Who are you?" he asked.
>
> "I am a king," said the beggar.
>
> "Where, then, is your kingdom?" asked Tauler.
>
> The beggar replied quietly, "In my heart."[8]

PRAYER OF FAITH

Find yourself a quiet corner. Still your heart. Come before Your heavenly Father with the innocence and faith of a little child. Picture Him as the generous Father who delights to provide good gifts to you. Take a few deep breaths. Every time you exhale, release every worry and anxiety that enters your mind. And, each time you inhale, thank Him for His goodness, kindness, and love for you. Take as long as you need. Let His peace fill and overwhelm your heart. Pray this prayer when you are ready:

> Lord, I choose to be anxious for nothing. I choose, in every-thing, to pray, to thank You, and to make my requests known

to You. I choose to believe in Your ability to provide for me even when I don't see it, feel it, or understand it. I choose to believe that if You can feed the birds of the air and clothe the flowers of the fields, surely You can provide for all my needs. I thank You that the peace of God, which surpasses all understanding, will guard my heart and mind through Jesus. Amen!

5

THE SPIRIT OF SONSHIP

"Slaves labor for provision; sons and daughters receive what
God has already made provision for."
—Cornelius Quek

When Paul speaks about sonship, he has in mind daughters as well.
Paul would say, *"There is neither male nor female; for you are all one
in Christ Jesus"* (Galatians 3:28). Sons and daughters, heirs, adopted
into the family of God—this is who we are when we receive Christ
into our lives. The day we were born again, we were set on this exhil-
arating journey of discovering who God is, who we are, and what we
have in God. When we better understand our identity as children of
God, dearly loved and cared for by our heavenly Father, we position
ourselves with confidence to receive the blessings that belong to us in
that covenant relationship.

The Bible often contrasts slavery and sonship. They are mutually
incompatible. Sons and daughters have privileges; slaves do not. *"A
slave has no permanent place in the family, but a son belongs to it forever"*
(John 8:35 NIV). Slaves and orphans are similar in that they labor for
something that they don't have—covering and belonging. Orphans
don't have parents, and slaves don't truly belong to anyone except the
masters they serve and labor for. Slaves labor for provision; sons and
daughters receive what God has already made provision for. I love
how *The Message* puts it:

> *You can tell for sure that you are now fully adopted as his own children because God sent the Spirit of his Son into our lives crying out, "Papa! Father!" Doesn't that privilege of intimate conversation with God make it plain that you are not a slave, but a child? And if you are a child, you're also an heir, with complete access to the inheritance.* (Galatians 4:6–7 MSG)

Perhaps no better example in the Bible reflects the theme of sonship than Luke 15:11–32, the parable of the prodigal son.

THE PRODIGAL FATHER

Many sermons have been preached about this parable, singling out the plight of the delinquent son. We would do the narrative injustice if we focused only on the wayward, younger son. The story is as much a characterization of the elder brother as the younger, as much a portrayal of the father as the two sons. The story begins with the younger son demanding a portion of the father's estate and inheritance, squandering it all on frivolous living, leading to the stark realization of his impoverishment and his eventual dramatic turnaround to come back home. The word *prodigal* is often taken to refer to someone who spends money or resources freely and recklessly, someone who is wastefully extravagant. However, it also refers to someone who is generous, lavish, and liberal in his giving.

The camera shifts from the son to the father—the prodigal father. After all, his treatment and reception of the younger son is as recklessly extravagant as he is generous and lavish. It just does not make sense. Just ask the older brother—he would never, in a million years, expect his dad to throw a welcome-home party with such a ridiculous display of festivity and opulence. He was so mad, he refused to acknowledge his brother in front of his father, and then not without a pejorative jibe: *"But as soon as this son of yours came, who has devoured your livelihood with harlots, you killed the fatted calf for him"* (Luke 15:30).

Though the son repented and decided to come back home, the Father took initiative to restore the family relationship. The Father gave his younger son the best robe, a ring, sandals, and a beautifully roasted fatted calf for dinner—an over-the-top demonstration of the father's openhandedness and unconditional acceptance. The best robe in the house would have been the father's robe. The father was covering and clothing the son with all of himself, with the best he could give. Sandals were a luxury in that day; servants did not wear them. The son was not to be treated as a slave. The father fully accepted and restored him. The wayward son was restored to full privileges.

> **THOSE WITH THE SPIRIT OF SONSHIP ACKNOWLEDGE THE FATHER AS THE SOURCE OF ALL PROVISION. THE SLAVE AND ORPHAN SPIRITS ARE INDEPENDENT, SELF-FOCUSED, AND OFTEN DETACHED FROM THE SOURCE.**

Provision was expended in the context of restored relationship and intimacy with the father. Relationship and intimacy always come first in our covenant relationship with the heavenly Father. Here's the principle—God's provision always occurs in the context of covenant relationship. We see that all throughout the Bible. God provides because He is in covenant relationship with His people. Unlike how we treat our covenant with God, God treats His covenant with His people with utmost consistency and fidelity. Think about the ten lepers whom Jesus healed. (See Luke 17:11–19.) Only one came back and acknowledged Jesus as the Healer. Those with the spirit of sonship acknowledge the Father as the Source of all provision. The slave and orphan spirits are independent, self-focused, and often detached from the Source.

THE "OLDER BROTHER" SYNDROME

Let's take a closer look at the older brother's response. Really, he didn't fare much better than the younger brother. He was alienated from the father in a different way.

Now his older son was in the field. And as he came and drew
near to the house, he heard music and dancing. So he called one
of the servants and asked what these things meant. And he said
to him, "Your brother has come, and because he has received him
safe and sound, your father has killed the fatted calf." "But he was
angry and would not go in. Therefore his father came out and
pleaded with him. So he answered and said to his father, "Lo,
these many years I have been serving you; I never transgressed
your commandment at any time; and yet you never gave me a
young goat, that I might make merry with my friends. But as soon
as this son of yours came, who has devoured your livelihood with
harlots, you killed the fatted calf for him." And he said to him,
"Son, you are always with me, and all that I have is yours. It was
right that we should make merry and be glad, for your brother
was dead and is alive again, and was lost and is found."

(Luke 15:25–32)

Let's backtrack a little and consider the context that Luke provides prior to Jesus's teaching. Two distinct groups of people had come to listen to Jesus. First, there were the *"tax collectors and the sinners"* (Luke 15:1), who perhaps, like the younger brother, lived waywardly and had no regard for moral living. Then there were the *"Pharisees and scribes"* (verse 2), who correspond to the older brother. They boast in their ability to hold on to and obey every law in Scripture. *Self-righteous* would be a good word to describe them. They were aghast that Jesus would welcome sinners and eat with them. (See Luke 15:2.) I imagine them thinking, *How dare He stoop down so low to eat with them. Has he even considered the ramifications of His actions? These sinners are going to think He accepts and approves of them! He's completely out of order!* The older brother must have felt very similar emotions, only directed toward his younger brother and his dad. Self-righteousness has a way of snuffing out the life in a relationship. It strips away intimacy, always puts oneself on the forefront, and pushes relationships and connections to the background.

The elder brother was hard at work in the field. He called it a day and made his way home. He heard the sound of music, dancing, and merrymaking. When he discovered that his delinquent brother had come home and was fully reinstated by his father, he was infuriated! The fact that he spoke to the servant first instead of going straight to his father reflected his lack of relationship and estrangement from him. He refused to partake in the celebration, possibly the greatest and most extravagant party the father had ever thrown. He stood outside the house, showing his disbelief and disgust at the father's actions. The father had to come out and plead with him to join in the celebrations, revealing the father's ungrudging heart. Nonetheless, the elder son's crotchety response was nothing but demeaning and dishonoring to the lord and father of the house.

> But he answered his father, "Look! All these years I've been slav-ing for you and never disobeyed your orders. Yet you never gave me even a young goat so I could celebrate with my friends. But when this son of yours who has squandered your property with prostitutes comes home, you kill the fattened calf for him!"
>
> (Luke 15:29–30 NIV)

The elder brother could not wrap his mind around the cost and the extravagance of it all. At this point, all he could think was that his dad was playing favorites, and he was seething at the injustice and unfair treatment.

Alright, let's do a little math and consider what this cost the elder brother. In Hebrew culture, when a father died, the oldest son received a double portion of the other children's inheritance. If a father had two children, the oldest would receive two-thirds of the estate and the younger would receive one-third. By restoring the younger son to full privileges in the family, the father was reinstat-ing his claim to one-third of the family's now very diminished estate. The father's extravagant treatment of the younger son was costing the older brother more than the cost of the fatted calf and party supplies. You can almost hear his words of fury: "What the heck? I've worked my butt off for you! I've obeyed you and done everything right! Where is the payoff? This good-for-nothing son of yours has done nothing for you and deserves only to be cast out from this family, and yet you lavish him with inexplicable generosity! Where is the justice in that?"

He saw himself as the model son; he did everything right. His problem wasn't what he did, for he certainly deserved credit for working hard. His issues were his attitude and the position from which he worked. *"All these years I've been slaving for you."* He was stuck in a slave mentality. He did not understand what being a son meant and the privileges that he had. His motto was, "You deserve what you put in. Nothing is free."

Now his fury has culminated to the point of utter disrespect and contempt for his father. He did not address his father appropriately and with honor, but simply said, *"Look!"* In that culture, when respect and deference to elders were expected, his behavior was appalling. How did the father respond to all of this? A man of that time and culture would have publicly castigated his son without hesitation. Instead, he responded with incredible magnanimity. The father sought restoration and connection, just as he had with the younger son.

> And he said to him, "Son, you are always with me, and all that I have is yours. It was right that we should make merry and be glad, for your brother was dead and is alive again, and was lost and is found." (Luke 15:31–32)

He called him *"son."* He reassured him that neither his actions nor the brother's return would in any way diminish his status. There had been no displacement of the elder son: His place at the father's house was as secure as ever, and his claim upon the family inheritance was in no way disturbed by this new development. The older brother should not have been bent out of shape because his younger brother had been blessed. You see, the spirit of sonship never gets envious or jealous when other siblings are celebrated. The spirit of sonship recognizes that God is the Source of all blessings, and He delights in blessing His children. God isn't rationing blessings because He's running low in His storehouses in heaven. He is the ultimate Blessing and Blesser!

> GOD ISN'T RATIONING BLESSINGS BECAUSE HE'S RUNNING
> LOW IN HIS STOREHOUSES IN HEAVEN.
> HE IS THE ULTIMATE BLESSING AND BLESSER!

Every good gift and every perfect gift is from above, and comes down from the Father of lights. (James 1:17)

The older son failed to recognize that the father delighted in providing for him. The father told him, *"All that I have is yours"* (Luke 15:31). As children of God, we get to partake of the Father's resources and blessings purely because of our status as a son and daughter, nothing else.

NO LONGER ORPHANS

Having an orphan spirit is a spiritual condition in which the believer's life source is cut off from the Father, resulting in a sense of abandonment, alienation, and isolation. By definition, an orphan is someone who does not have parents. The orphan spirit is fatherless, homeless, rebellious, reckless, and independent. The orphan spirit operates and is motivated by strife and performance to merit God's blessing and provision. It runs against the concept of grace. Grace, or the unmerited favor of God, does not disregard biblical concepts like hard work, diligence, stewardship, and responsibility; but it acknowledges that, even on our best days, we cannot earn the blessings of God.

I grew up in an Asian family in Singapore, where the underlying motivation and drive was to perform and excel. As a kid, if I came home from school with a B on my report card, I'd get smacked by my dad. But if I came home with an A, my dad would take me shopping for nice and expensive clothing and gifts. I remember my parents saying to me, "If you don't work, you don't eat. No one is going to provide for you. You must fend for yourself. Every man for himself." It is no wonder I operated in independence, self-sufficiency, performance, and strife as I grew into an adult.

When I became a Christian at sixteen, this unhealthy strife and performance began to affect the way I viewed God the Father. I saw Him as a harsh slave master who only rewarded and blessed me if I kept every rule and did everything right. Let me share with you a personal journey of how it affected the way I saw how God would provide a spouse for me. In my prayer and journey in trusting God for a spouse, I believed that God would not let me meet my wife until I had everything right in my life, if my ducks were in a row, if I had crossed all my t's and dotted all my i's. For some people, that might sound ridiculous. Perhaps some of you can relate. I believed that I wasn't married because I wasn't good enough, holy enough, or pure enough. I held on to that belief for many years.

Eventually, I saw a Christian counselor and shared with him how angry I was with God because He hadn't provided a wife for me. I had kept myself pure by not dating for twelve years! Where was the payoff? I was just like the older brother in the story. I obeyed because really, deep down, I wanted to be married, not because I wanted to delight and please God. I remember, during the counseling session, I saw a mental picture of myself cleaning out the closet in my room. I was scrubbing it, wiping it down, making sure there were no specks of dust or cobwebs before I proceeded to put my clothing in. I shared that with my counselor, as well as my experience growing up. He shared that he felt that I was stuck in performance and strife. It confirmed the lie that I had believed in those years—that God was withholding my wife from me because I hadn't cleaned up everything and gotten my act together. We broke and renounced that lie that day.

> THERE ARE BLESSINGS IN OBEYING GOD AND LIVING RIGHT
> BEFORE HIM. HE REWARDS OUR OBEDIENCE.
> WE CANNOT EARN HIS BLESSING BY MERIT.

There are blessings in obeying God and living right before Him. He rewards our obedience. We cannot earn His blessing by merit. In the parable, both brothers sought to receive the father's blessings. Neither of them cared for a relationship or connection with the father. Both wanted the blessings and the wealth but not the father. Both wanted things done their own way. They both rebelled, one by being very bad and the other by being extremely good. Neither worked. God's blessings and provision are not conditional on how good or bad we are. His grace breaks through every limitation. Provision always takes place in the context of a father-son relationship, connection, intimacy, and dependence.

Maybe some of you are stuck in the same rut as I was. You are stuck in the performance mode. "I am not good enough, I've got to be better. I'm not holy enough. I've got to pray more, fast more..." Stop! You can't earn His blessings. You can certainly please God with your faith and obedience, but you can't earn His goodness, kindness, and generosity. That would sabotage and nullify all that Jesus did on the cross on your behalf. When we see ourselves less than how God sees us, we make a mockery of the grace of God. Renounce the orphan spirit and every God-limiting and self-limiting lie that is robbing you of God's provision for your life!

I will not leave you orphans; I will come to you. (John 14:18)

Paul is the only author in the New Testament to use the word *"adoption,"* the Greek word *hyiothesia*, which literally means "placing as a son."[1] It is a legal term that describes the process by which a man brings another person into his family, the implication of which is that person gets to enjoy the status and privileges of a biological son or daughter. We are adopted into the family of God when we become "in Christ." It is one of the spiritual privileges and blessings God has bestowed on us.

Blessed be the God and Father of our Lord Jesus Christ, who has blessed us with every spiritual blessing in the heavenly places in Christ...having predestined us to adoption as sons by Jesus Christ to Himself, according to the good pleasure of His will.
(Ephesians 1:3, 5)

It is the Father's good pleasure to adopt us as His own. Through the Spirit of adoption, we get to call God our Abba, Father. Not only have our statuses been changed from slaves to sons and daughters, we have become heirs of God and co-heirs with Christ!

> *Because you are sons, God has sent forth the Spirit of His Son into your hearts, crying out, "Abba, Father!" Therefore you are no longer a slave but a son, and if a son, then an heir of God through Christ.* (Galatians 4:6–7)

> *For you did not receive the spirit of bondage again to fear, but you received the Spirit of adoption by whom we cry out, "Abba, Father." The Spirit Himself bears witness with our spirit that we are children of God, and if children, then heirs—heirs of God and joint heirs with Christ.* (Romans 8:15–17)

We have also become heirs of the promises given to Abraham. *"If you are Christ's, then you are Abraham's seed, and heirs according to the promise"* (Galatians 3:29). This is in line with the foundation I discussed in chapter 1, "May I Be Cursed if I Do Not Provide for You." As Abraham's seed then, we also inherit Abraham's promise, that is, a relationship with God that is characterized by God's covenant provision.

THE SIGNIFICANCE OF JESUS, THE FIRSTBORN

The term *firstborn* has two meanings. The first is more literal, referring to Jesus as the firstborn Son. Jesus was Mary's firstborn. The second meaning refers to a person who is the firstborn, with all the rights and authority of that designation. Jesus was also the firstborn of His heavenly Father, *"the firstborn over all creation"* (Colossians 1:15). He was not first in the sense of time, but He was supreme in power and authority over all creation. In addition, Jesus was identified as the firstborn among the *"assembly...of the firstborn"* (Hebrews 12:23), among the whole family of God, who is destined to bear His image. Scripture says,

> *For whom He foreknew, He also predestined to be conformed to the image of His Son, that He might be the firstborn among many brethren.* (Romans 8:29)

In other words, as Christ is the firstborn, so are we firstborn spiritually by God's grace. Scripture is clear that we share in Christ and what He does. We are *"partakers of the divine nature"* (2 Peter 1:4). We are "seated with Christ in the heavenly places." (See Ephesians 2:6.). The works that Christ does, we will do also. (See John 14:12.) It is through our relationship with Christ, who is the Firstborn par excellence, that we have become the firstborn heirs of God. Now, as brothers and sisters in Christ, we get to share in the blessings that He has secured for us.

> IT IS THROUGH OUR RELATIONSHIP WITH CHRIST, WHO IS THE FIRSTBORN PAR EXCELLENCE, THAT WE HAVE BECOME THE FIRSTBORN HEIRS OF GOD. NOW, AS BROTHERS AND SISTERS IN CHRIST, WE GET TO SHARE IN THE BLESSINGS THAT HE HAS SECURED FOR US.

In the Jewish culture, when a father passed away, his firstborn son would receive a double portion of the family's inheritance. (See Deuteronomy 21:17.) In Israel and the rest of the ancient world, the firstborn son enjoyed a favored and privileged position. Moreover, the firstborn's benefits included a special blessing from the father involving material prosperity. (See Genesis 27:28.) Isn't it prophetic then that, when Christ died, we as the firstborn in the family of God, as sons and daughters and heirs of the promises, get to inherit everything that Christ has made provision for?

> He who did not spare His own Son, but delivered Him up for us all, how shall He not with Him also freely give us all things?
> (Romans 8:32)

WE GET TO CALL HIM "ABBA"

The first and perhaps most important thing Jesus taught His disciples to pray was to address God as "Abba." *"Our [Abba] in heaven…*

Give us this day our daily bread" (Matthew 6:9, 11). In this short petition is an invitation to relationship and covenant provision. Jesus revolutionized the way in which the disciples approached God from then on. God was not just the political Messiah they were expecting to deliver Israel; Jesus called Him their Father, their Abba. The Aramaic term *abba* reflects a loving dependent relationship between a child and a father.

In Jewish culture, *abba* was a term of special affection and intimacy used by children to address their earthly fathers, showing security and confidence in their father's providential care. As Abba, God is a Father who provides for the needs of His children. He is the One in heaven, all-powerful and more than able to provide. By teaching the disciples to call God "Abba," Jesus was introducing covenant language. Jesus presented a whole new level of intimacy. That was the key to the prayer. Jesus was inviting them to a level of relationship with the Father just as He had. And because God is their Father, they could count on Him to provide. When we recognize the benevolence of a loving Father, we understand and are confident that all our needs will be met.

> RELATIONSHIP AND INTIMACY IS THE LANGUAGE OF GOD'S HEART. IF GOD WERE JUST A STRONG PROVIDER WITH NO INTENTION TO CONNECT WITH THOSE HE MADE, HE WOULD HAVE CREATED JUST THE EARTH FILLED WITH AWESOME NATURE, NOT RELATIONAL HUMAN BEINGS WITH FEELINGS AND A LONGING FOR CONNECTION.

Growing up, my dad was a strong provider. We always had food on the table and nice clothes to wear. However, he was emotionally absent. In fact, he did not tell me he loved me until I was in my later twenties. I stood frozen like a Popsicle. I didn't know how to respond. It felt awkwardly unfamiliar. I never felt connected to him until my mid-thirties. I knew my dad as a father but not as a friend. His provision for the family was tied to his role, not his connection to my brother and me. I didn't doubt his love for us, but I never felt it. In many ways, I felt like an orphan; places in my heart felt dead.

Relationship and intimacy is the language of God's heart. If God were just a strong provider with no intention to connect with those He made, He would have created just the earth filled with awesome nature, not relational human beings with feelings and a longing for connection. He wants to relate and connect with us, not just provide for us. The longer I walk with the Lord, the more I realize I need to understand His heart as my father, not just His role, knowing who He is and not just what He does. In knowing His heart, we find meaning and significance to all that He does and provides for us. When we don't understand His heart, we will default to a lifeless, mechanical relationship.

HONORING YOUR PARENTS RELEASES THE BLESSINGS

In Western society, honoring parents has not only become an archaic and obsolete concept, but is frowned upon and deemed valueless by some. In the consumerist society, in which individualism is highly valued, people think and act selfishly, and do not consider others' preference, including their own parents'. Sadly, Christians haven't fared much better in obeying this commandment. God, in His divine wisdom, has designed His people to reap great benefits and blessings by honoring their parents. I want to show you how honoring our parents can trigger the provision of God in our lives.

The fifth commandment reads, *"Honor your father and your mother"* (Exodus 20:12). It is also interesting that the commandment not only made its way to the top ten laws, but it is on the right tablet, the side concerned with the relationship between God and us. The first commandment states, *"I am [Adonai] your God"* (verse 2). The second is, *"You shall have no other gods before Me"* (verse 3). Third, *"You shall not make for yourself a carved image [of Me or any living thing]"* (verse 4). And, fourth, *"Remember the Sabbath day, to keep it holy"* (verse 8). And then, *"Honor your father and mother, that your days may be long upon the land which [Adonai] is giving you"* (verse 12). One would expect it to be on the left tablet with its laws concerning how humans do business with each other—"*You shall not murder. You shall not commit adultery. You shall not steal. You shall not bear false witness against your neighbor. You shall not covet...anything that is your neighbor's*" (Exodus 20:13–17). On the contrary, it is found right after the law to keep the Sabbath.

The first four commandments deal with laws between man and God. The last five deal with laws between man and man. The commandment to honor the parents bridges the gap, but it is classified as a commandment between man and God, not man and man.[2] Most people would classify honoring one's parents as the latter. The Jewish people were being taught that they should view serving their parents as tantamount to serving God.[3] In other words, a person's relationship with his parents directly affects his relationship with God. Remarkably, this is one of the few commandments that offers a reward.

> *Children, obey your parents in the Lord, for this is right. "Honor your father and mother," which is the first commandment with a promise: "that it may be well with you and you may live long on the earth."* (Ephesians 6:1–3)

A few years ago, I traveled to Singapore to visit my dad, my brother, and his family. One morning, while I was having my time with the Lord, the Holy Spirit brought to my mind the promise in Ephesians 6:1–3. I always knew the promise of longevity if I chose to honor my parents, but the Spirit brought to my attention the words "*that it may be well with you*" (Ephesians 6:3). Then He whispered to my spirit, "Son, honoring your parents is a key to your success." He directed me to Malachi 4:5–6:

> *Behold, I will send you Elijah the prophet before the coming of the great and dreadful day of the LORD. And he will turn the hearts of the fathers to the children, and the hearts of the children to their fathers, lest I come and strike the earth with a curse.*

What struck me from this Scripture is that, in the last days, the avoidance of the curse of the land is conditional upon the reconciliation and bonding of hearts between fathers and children. In other words, the prosperity of the land is connected to the way in which fathers relate with their children and children with their father.

During that period, I had been contending to be debt free. The Holy Spirit instructed me to sow financially to my dad. I murmured in my heart, *Lord, I am a missionary. You know I do not have much, but I know You are speaking to me. I will give to my dad. How much?* The Lord revealed an amount to me. It wasn't much, but I knew it was significant. That morning, I went to my dad, who was a Buddhist at that time (he later gave his life to Jesus!).

"Dad, here's a little something for you," I said as I handed him a red envelope (red is a color of blessing in Asian culture) with the money in it.

"Son, you are the one who needs this money. Keep it."

"Dad, you do not understand. You need to keep it."

The next day, I received a random text from my friend's mom in Tulsa, Oklahoma: "Cornelius, I am sending you three thousand dollars today."

I was stunned. I was amazed that I did not know this lady well, and God had laid it on her heart to give generously to me.

The next day, I was driving in the car with my good friend Chris, and I began to tell him about the generous gift I had received the day before. Chris grinned from ear to ear as if he knew something I was clueless about.

"Why are you grinning so happily?"

"Wait till you get to my house. I have something to give to you," Chris replied.

When we got to Chris's house, he disappeared into his room and came out with an envelope in his hand.

"Here you go—this is yours. A few of the guys got together and decided to bless you."

I had a feeling it was a financial gift, but I was not ready for the amount that was in the envelope. I opened it up and saw a stack of one-thousand-dollar bills. Two days after the Lord had spoken to me about the promise of honoring my parents, *"that it might go well with you,"* my entire debt was paid off, with spare change!

I am careful not to make this sound like a surefire, genie-in-a-bottle formula to be prosperous. This is not a promise that you will be debt-free if you choose to honor your parents financially. God promised that we will do well and be blessed if we choose to honor our parents. Maybe that will look like a restored relationship with your parents, healing in your body, a raise and promotion at your job, or an immediate download of a business idea. God's blessings are diverse and endless. He knows how to bless us and provide for us. He is a good heavenly Father. You will do well to honor your parents regardless of whether they deserve it or not, because when you do, you honor God. And when we honor Him, we will be blessed. I encourage you to ask the Holy Spirit how you can honor your parents. He will show you!

PRAYER OF FAITH

Thank You, Father, for calling us sons and daughters. Thank You that I am no longer a slave or an orphan. I no longer have to strive to earn Your blessings, but I get to feast at the table You have prepared before me. Thank You, Father, that I am abundantly satisfied with the fullness of Your house and that I get to drink from the river of Your pleasures. Surely, goodness and mercy will follow me the rest of my days. Thank You, Abba. Amen!

6

DEPENDENCY IS OUR POSTURE

"If we really fully belong to God, then we must be at His
disposal and we must trust in Him.
We must never be preoccupied with the future.
There is no reason to be. God is there."[1]
—Mother Teresa

Learning to trust God to provide for our needs is a stretch for most
people. It is not a whole lot of fun to be vulnerable, to be at the mercy
of uncertainty. Despite the promises of God, many of us struggle
with the nebulous concept of trusting someone we can't see. Will
God provide? What do I have to do? What if He doesn't show up?
Can He be trusted? We love to sit in the driving seat of our lives and
circumstances. The thought of not being in control is enough to cause
a cold sweat. It makes us nauseous. It is uncomfortable.

Everyone needs provision, but not everyone has learned how to
depend on God for it. However, it is the only way to live in the kingdom of God.

> But seek first the kingdom of God and His righteousness, and all
> these things shall be added to you.   (Matthew 6:33)

We are primed for God's provision when we are preoccupied
with His priorities. That is how God has wired us. We were created

to seek the Father and depend on Him for everything. Independence and self-reliance are not part of our makeup. We were designed to experience His provision simply because we are His children. To know and experience the heart of the good Father is our reward this side of heaven. Jesus taught us to pray, *"Give us this day our daily bread"* (Matthew 6:11). He wouldn't have said that unless He planned on answering it. God is not a teaser.

WE ARE PRIMED FOR GOD'S PROVISION WHEN WE ARE PREOCCUPIED WITH HIS PRIORITIES.

FAITH IN THE CHARACTER OF GOD

Hebrews 11 is such a gem, highlighting many biblical heroes of faith. Many of these champions had to learn the ways of faith in their unique journeys and experiences with God. Faith is a powerful key that releases the resources of heaven. Scripture talks about the kind of faith that pleases God:

> *It's impossible to please God apart from faith. And why? Because anyone who wants to approach God must believe both that he exists and that he cares enough to respond to those who seek him.* (Hebrews 11:6 MSG)

The faith that pleases God and releases His provision is the faith that believes in all God says He is. The power of faith releases the essence and attributes of God to meet our every need. This faith *"believes that he exists and that he cares enough to respond."* Some of you need to stop believing the lie that God has more important things to take care of in the world than your needs, or that He's always attending to the needs of others instead of yours. If it matters to you, it matters to Him. How you see Him will determine how you see your circumstances. Faith demands that you match your thoughts about God and His character with His thoughts about you and your circumstances.

HOW YOU SEE GOD WILL DETERMINE HOW YOU SEE YOUR CIRCUMSTANCES. FAITH DEMANDS THAT YOU MATCH YOUR THOUGHTS ABOUT GOD AND HIS CHARACTER WITH HIS THOUGHTS ABOUT YOU AND YOUR CIRCUMSTANCES.

Moses was called by God to deliver the people of Israel. Moses was not only insecure in his ability but unconvinced of the One who had called and sent him.

> *Then Moses said to God, "Indeed, when I come to the children of Israel and say to them, 'The God of your fathers has sent me to you,' and they say to me, 'What is His name?' what shall I say to them?" And God said to Moses, "I AM WHO I AM." And He said, "Thus you shall say to the children of Israel, 'I AM has sent me to you.'"* (Exodus 3:13–14)

The Israelites' question *"What is His name?"* has little to do with identity, for they would have been familiar with *"the God of your fathers."* They would surely understand that Moses was referring to none other than the God of their fathers, Abraham, Isaac, and Jacob. Moses' question about God's name had to do more with God's reputation, whether He could accomplish what He was promising. God identifies Himself as *"I AM WHO I AM."* How many of you would think that's a random and bizarre way of introducing yourself? It would be just as bizarre if you met somebody at a party and he introduced himself as "I Am the Dancer of the Dances." (Don't ever introduce yourself that way if you ever want to score a date.) Only God could get away with a nebulous introduction like that. Many words describe the nature of God. He is holy, merciful, kind, the Alpha and Omega, the Provider, and so much more. All of God's names testify to His reputation. But the name *"I AM WHO I AM"* encapsulates and epitomizes the fullness of God and who He is. The reality is that no one name could fully capture the essence of who He is. He is that profound!

God, in revealing His divine name to Moses, declared and prophesied His character and attributes to the immediate situation. The issue at hand was not so much who Moses was but, more importantly, who was with him. The Hebrew word signifying *"I AM WHO I AM"* carries the meaning "to be." It points to the absolute existence of God. It suggests a continuing, unfinished action: "I am being that I am being" or "the one who always is."[2] It would be inappropriate to refer to Him as "was" or "will be," for He is the "now," the "present" God. He is not an abstract being so far removed from our experience. He is not lagging so far behind you or blazing so far ahead of you that He cannot connect and relate to your current needs and situations. Faith is the confidence that God acts in the "now." He knows your needs. He cares for you. He is with you!

SABBATH AND JUBILEE—THE HEART OF DEPENDENCE

In Leviticus 25, God gave Moses instructions concerning the keeping of the Sabbath and the year of Jubilee. The laws of God were never intended to steal our fun and joy; they were meant to benefit us. God's not the celestial party pooper that most people think. Only a benevolent and generous God could put our welfare and interests before His at all times. The heart behind keeping the Sabbath and Jubilee was to bring God's people to a place of utter dependence on His ability, capacity, and delight to provide for His children. To understand the year of Jubilee more clearly, we must first understand the concept of the Sabbath. What is the significance of the Sabbath that is listed in the Ten Commandments? It is the longest of all the commandments and is placed even before the moral commandments, such as *"You shall not murder"* (Exodus 20:13) and *"You shall not steal"* (Exodus 20:15).

The Sabbath embodies the heart and provision of the gospel. Central to the message of the gospel is that God the Father made provision. He gave His Son to take care of the eternal problem of sin and separation between God and man, once and for all. We have earned and deserved nothing. We are dependent on God. Without Him, we are doomed.

And the LORD spoke to Moses on Mount Sinai, saying, "Speak to the children of Israel, and say to them: 'When you come into the land which I give you, then the land shall keep a sabbath to the LORD. Six years you shall sow your field, and six years you shall prune your vineyard, and gather its fruit; but in the seventh year there shall be a sabbath of solemn rest for the land, a sabbath to the LORD. You shall neither sow your field nor prune your vineyard. What grows of its own accord of your harvest you shall not reap, nor gather the grapes of your untended vine, for it is a year of rest for the land. And the sabbath produce of the land shall be food for you: for you, your male and female servants, your hired man, and the stranger who dwells with you, for your livestock and the beasts that are in your land—all its produce shall be for food.   (Leviticus 25:1–7)

God's Sabbath instructions to Moses extended to the land itself. A Sabbath for the land was to take place every seventh year. The Israelites were to work the land for six years and, on the seventh year, neither sow nor prune. The land had to be free from toil; it had to rest. The Lord's attentiveness and foresight in ensuring that the Israelites were provided for are reflected in the land's yield after six years—it was more than sufficient to sustain life during the seventh year. The list of the seven recipients of the produce of the land—*"you, your male and female servants, your hired man, and the stranger who dwells with you, for your livestock and the beasts that are in your land"* (Leviticus 25:6–7)—indicates God's foreknowledge, intention, wisdom, and capacity to provide for everything that concerns His people. The people had no fear of lack.

The sabbatical year extends to seven seven-year cycles, which culminates in the fiftieth year with the celebration of the year of Jubilee.

That fiftieth year shall be a Jubilee to you; in it you shall neither sow nor reap what grows of its own accord, nor gather the grapes of your untended vine. For it is the Jubilee; it shall be holy to you; you shall eat its produce from the field.   (Leviticus 25:11–12)

So you shall observe My statutes and keep My judgments, and perform them; and you will dwell in the land in safety. Then the land will yield its fruit, and you will eat your fill, and dwell there in safety. And if you say, "What shall we eat in the seventh year, since we shall not sow nor gather in our produce?" Then I will command My blessing on you in the sixth year, and it will bring forth produce enough for three years. And you shall sow in the eighth year, and eat old produce until the ninth year; until its produce comes in, you shall eat of the old harvest.

(Leviticus 25:18–22)

In the year of Jubilee, just like the sabbatical year, the people could eat only what had been harvested from the fields. This year followed the seventh sabbatical year, which meant that the land had been fallow for two consecutive years. This arrangement obviously would have been a severe test of faith for the Israelites. Again, this reflects God's original design to draw us to a place of intimacy and utter dependence on Him for our provision. We've been invited into a deep relationship with the Creator and Sustainer of the universe, in which we get to trust and experience Yahweh's profound ability to provide for our necessities in life.

The caveat was their obedience and complete dependence on Him. If the Israelites complied with God's requirements, they didn't have to worry about what they would eat in the sabbatical year. God ensured that they would be securely and adequately provided for. (See Leviticus 8:18–19.) Moreover, if the Israelites were faithful to God's commands, God would send such an abundance of blessing in the sixth year of the cycle that the land would yield enough food for three years. The yield would be so great that it would continue until two years after the sabbatical year. (See Leviticus 8:21–22.) God promised abundant food for which the Israelites did not have to toil. They had to believe God from a place of rest and trust. This is reminiscent of another event when God provided manna for the Sabbath day. (See Exodus 16.) You have to take your hat off to a genius God who had a plan and strategy in place for provision. God is incapable of *not* providing. He loves and cares for His children too much for that.

Here are a few key implications. *"The earth is the* Lord's, *and everything in it"* (Psalm 24:1 NLT). He owns *"the cattle on a thousand hills"* (Psalm 50:10). He is a God of abundance, and God is Provider of all. The provision of crops did not depend on man's labor and toil but on God as the Sustainer. Work and labor are important, but God is the ultimate source and provider of all our needs. Lastly, God is looking for willing hearts who depend on Him wholeheartedly. Obedience and dependence on God are the one-two punch that attracts God's blessings and provision.

STRIPPED DOWN FAITH

In Judges 7, God sent Gideon to save Israel from the hand of the Midianites.

> *And the* Lord *said to Gideon, "The people who are with you are too many for Me to give the Midianites into their hands, lest Israel claim glory for itself against Me, saying, 'My own hand has saved me.' Now therefore, proclaim in the hearing of the people, saying, 'Whoever is fearful and afraid, let him turn and depart at once from Mount Gilead.'" And twenty-two thousand of the people returned, and ten thousand remained.*
>
> (Judges 7:2–3)

God has a way of showing His people that He alone gets the glory for everything. He is not a narcissistic, egotistical God who is needy and craves attention. Rather, He knows that our becoming prideful and self-sufficient hinders our relationship with Him and impedes His provision in our lives. He wants us to hold on to that rope of dependence on Him, tight and secure.

Gideon's army started with thirty-two thousand men. Twenty-two thousand were fearful and afraid. Intimidation filled the atmosphere. Nobody wanted to die. Nobody wanted to lose his family. The first cut reduced the army to ten thousand. The faith and courage of Gideon and the ten thousand had to be wearing thin at that point. Jelly knees, wet pants, stripped down faith. Then the unimaginable happened.

*But the L*ORD *said to Gideon, "The people are still too many;*
bring them down to the water, and I will test them for you there.
Then it will be, that of whom I say to you, 'This one shall go with
you,' the same shall go with you; and of whomever I say to you,
'This one shall not go with you,' the same shall not go."

(Judges 7:4)

Ten thousand men were reduced to three hundred.

*Then the L*ORD *said to Gideon, "By the three hundred men who*
lapped I will save you, and deliver the Midianites into your
hand."   (verse 7)

The enemies were "*as numerous as locusts; and their camels were*
without number, as the sand by the seashore in multitude." (verse 12).
Three hundred Israelites versus the multitudes of the enemies. In
the natural, it was a walkover. If their pants weren't wet before, they
would have been now. With whatever faith and courage they had left,
they stood their ground, holding on to the torches in their left hands
and trumpets in their right, as they waited for Gideon's instructions.
And then the unimaginable happened. This time, when they blew
their trumpets and cried, "*The sword of the L*ORD *and of Gideon!*"
(Judges 7:18), the Lord confused their enemies and caused them to
kill one another!

*When the three hundred blew the trumpets, the L*ORD *set every*
man's sword against his companion throughout the whole camp;
and the army fled to Beth Acacia, toward Zererah, as far as the
border of Abel Meholah, by Tabbath.   (Judges 7:22)

SOMETIMES GOD HAS TO STRIP YOU DOWN TO YOUR BARE BONES TO GIVE YOU THE MEAT OF YOUR VICTORY. HE DOESN'T DO IT TO TEASE OR FRUSTRATE US. HE GETS NO PLEASURE FROM SEEING US IN LACK.

Here's the lesson. Sometimes God has to strip you down to your bare bones to give you the meat of your victory. He doesn't do it to tease or frustrate us. He gets no pleasure from seeing us in lack. I used to have a golden retriever named Glory. I used to dangle a treat above his head for extended periods of time just to see how he would respond—how hungry he was for my "blessing." And I did it shamelessly and purely for my entertainment. Aren't you glad I am not God? God is not sitting on His golden throne in heaven, sipping on "heavenade," enjoying watching how frustrated we are because of lack. But He does want our absolute dependence. Why? Because, in surrender and trust, we truly get to know His heart and His power to provide.

> Don't let the wise boast in their wisdom, or the powerful boast in their power, or the rich boast in their riches. But those who wish to boast should boast in this alone: that they truly know me and understand that I am the LORD who demonstrates unfailing love. (Jeremiah 9:23–24 NLT)

Nothing pleases a father more than when his children know his heart and love for them. I imagine that nothing excites God more than His children knowing and experiencing His generous nature. I believe that we get to experience His provision to the degree we understand the revelation of His lovingkindness toward us.

ASK, SEEK, KNOCK

The Word of God is the road map to the heart of the Father, and worship and prayer is the vehicle that leads us there. Some years ago, I was learning about the prayers of Jesus at seminary. The Lord spoke to me clearly, "Prayer is knowing Me, not just asking Me." If our priorities in prayer are not to seek and understand the heart of the Father, we cut ourselves short of the true value of prayer. When we understand His heart, we understand His will. When we understand and pray His will, we position ourselves to receive all He's intended for us. Yes, we should ask, petition, request, and supplicate—the Bible teaches us to do all those things—but we cannot let our requests, concerns, and needs overshadow the Lord Himself.

> *Now this is the confidence that we have in Him, that if we ask anything according to His will, He hears us. And if we know that He hears us, whatever we ask, we know that we have the petitions that we have asked of Him.* (1 John 5:14–15)

The key to asking is asking according to His will. What is His will? What's in His heart. How do we know His heart? By reading the Word of God and allowing the Holy Spirit to breathe life and revelation into our unique circumstances and needs. I understand that the Bible doesn't tell us which college to go to or which job to apply for. His will never violates His heart, and His heart never violates His will. When we know the Father's heart, we will have the revelation of His will and guidance in our decisions.

The Bible teaches us to ask, seek, and knock as we approach God in prayer for His provision. Elsewhere, in the Lord's Prayer, Jesus taught us to ask for our daily bread. On both accounts, our asking is in the context of a Father–Son relationship. Therefore, our posture when we pray and ask of the Father as sons and daughters cannot be undermined.

> *So I say to you, ask, and it will be given to you; seek, and you will find; knock, and it will be opened to you. For everyone who asks receives, and he who seeks finds, and to him who knocks it will be opened. If a son asks for bread from any father among you, will he give him a stone? Or if he asks for a fish, will he give him a serpent instead of a fish? Or if he asks for an egg, will he offer him a scorpion? If you then, being evil, know how to give good gifts to your children, how much more will your heavenly Father give the Holy Spirit to those who ask Him!* (Luke 11:9–13)

> *Your Father knows the things you have need of before you ask Him. In this manner, therefore, pray: Our Father in heaven,*

*hallowed be Your name. Your kingdom come. Your will be done
on earth as it is in heaven. Give us this day our daily bread.*

(Matthew 6:8–11)

"Ask," *"seek,"* and *"knock"* are in the Greek present tense, implying continued action.[3] Jesus is encouraging persevering prayer with
an attitude of filial trust. We don't need to beg God, but He desires
constant connection and fellowship with His children. Jesus reminds
us of the nature of the One to whom we are praying. In this passage,
the fatherhood of God is being compared to human fatherhood. The
profound difference is that God responds to our requests with more
pertinence and generosity than we do to the requests of our children.
Here Jesus used a qal wahomer to accentuate the caring love of the
Father.[4] If imperfect human parents know how to nurture the real
needs of their children, how much more can we expect our heavenly
Father to bless us with the Holy Spirit! (See Luke 11:13. The parallel
account in Matthew 7:11 says, *"Good things."*)

I have read this account in Luke many times and have often won-
dered why Luke highlighted the blessing of the Holy Spirit from the
Father, whereas Matthew highlighted *"good things"* from the Father.
It seems random and out of place. Was Luke trying to substitute the
Holy Spirit in place of *"good things"?* Are they mutually exclusive?
James 1:17 says, *"Every good gift and every perfect gift is from above,"*
and Romans 8:32 says, *"How shall He not with Him also freely give us
all things?"* No doubt the Father wants to bless us with good things.
That's not the issue. The point Luke was trying to emphasize was
that the Father has blessed us with the best gift, the Holy Spirit. The
gift of the Holy Spirit as God's highest gift to mankind should give
us every confidence that the good Father will not hold back anything
that we need.

HE ALREADY KNOWS YOUR NEEDS

*And when you pray, do not use vain repetitions as the heathen
do. For they think that they will be heard for their many words.*

Therefore do not be like them. For your Father knows the things
you have need of before you ask Him. (Matthew 6:7–8)

I practice all kinds of prayers. Declarative prayers, thanksgiving prayers, silent prayers, and reflective and contemplative prayers. But the kind of prayer that God seems to have an aversion to is wordy prayers. Hey, I'm cool with that! As a man, I have a seven-thousand-word quota on any given day anyway! Jesus is not against words. Words are important and powerful, and they can communicate the deepest feelings. However, Jesus is not a fan of pompous, circumlocutory, periphrastic, tautological ramblings. You get the picture. Effective prayers are not showy or formulaic; they are humble and dependent, and come from the heart that longs to connect with the Father. One of my favorite things to do in my relationship with God is thinking prayers. No words. Just submitting my thoughts, praise, thanksgiving, concerns, and requests to the Lord. It's all about the connection.

> **EFFECTIVE PRAYERS ARE NOT SHOWY OR FORMULAIC;**
> **THEY ARE HUMBLE AND DEPENDENT, AND COME FROM THE HEART**
> **THAT LONGS TO CONNECT WITH THE FATHER.**

Have you ever wondered why we need to ask for our needs when God already knows them? I mean, is God amnesic? Is He so busy with saving the world that He expects me to remind Him lest He forget? I am all about maximizing time and effort and being effective. "Lord, if you already know my needs, then let's cut to the chase. You just go ahead and do what You have to do to take care of all my needs. Thank You very much!"

Two schools of thought help to explain this. Believers tend to swing to one or the other. On one hand, divine determinism says that, if God is sovereign and has already determined to do as He wills, then prayer is futile and unnecessary. Take, for example, the issue of healing. This camp believes that, if a person gets sick and God has willed it, then no amount of prayer can alter it. Sickness, then, is fatalistic, and that person is to accept it. By the same token, if God wills healing, then it will become a reality with or without prayer. The other end of the pendulum places its confidence in a faith formula. Its dependence is on human faith and confession rather than on the divine power of God. American optimism has blended with Christian fundamentalism to generate a triumphalistic theological hybrid that is both attractive and precarious. According to this, a person could "faith" or "confess" his way to healing, provision, and answers to prayers. If healing doesn't happen, their faith didn't work.

This begs the question: Is God sovereign, and is faith confession relevant? The answer is yes. The heart of the matter is dependency. If God is sovereign and prayer is irrelevant, then our dependency is irrelevant. In addition, there is power in faith declaration, but our faith is not in faith. Our dependency is on the immutable, benevolent, loving character and nature of God. Prayer, in essence, is knowing God. Prayer must not only bring us to our knees to say, "I need You, Lord," but pull on our heart's affections to say, "I must know You more."

If the Father knows your needs before you utter them, and words don't seem to matter the most in prayer, then articulation isn't the most significant part of prayer. Agreement, not articulation, is what brings heaven to earth and answers to prayers. Faith, in its most salient meaning, is agreement with God about who He is, and what He says about you and your needs. I have learned to pray not based on my needs but on the unchanging nature and goodness of my good Father. The question is not if He knows your needs—He already does—the question is if you know who He is.

Words from your mouth express your heart and needs, but agreement with His divine nature and will rivets heaven's attention and releases its resources.

Therefore, pray this way:

- "Lord, I agree with heaven concerning my health. Release heaven's healing!"

+ "Lord, I agree with heaven concerning my financial needs. Release heaven's supply according to Your riches in glory!"

+ "Lord, I agree with heaven concerning my prodigal son/daughter. Release the angels of heaven to bring him/her home!"

+ "Lord, let Your kingdom come, Your will be done!"

ACTION FOLLOWS AGREEMENT

> *In the same way, faith by itself, if it is not accompanied by action, is dead.* (James 2:17 NIV)

Actions must follow agreement with God. Many pray for more faith. Sometimes, that's not what we need. We need to act and put feet to our faith. We need to act on the measure of faith that we've already received through God's grace. Listen to the Holy Spirit, stand on the promises of God, and act on what He is saying to you concerning your needs. Here's a cool testimony about that.

> **WE NEED TO ACT ON THE MEASURE OF FAITH THAT WE'VE ALREADY RECEIVED THROUGH GOD'S GRACE. LISTEN TO THE HOLY SPIRIT, STAND ON THE PROMISES OF GOD, AND ACT ON WHAT HE IS SAYING TO YOU CONCERNING YOUR NEEDS.**

As I've mentioned before, I attended the Discipleship Training School with Youth with a Mission Singapore years ago. I knew the Lord had told me to do it. The only problem was that I didn't have the money for it. I showed up at the mission base on the first day of school and, honestly, I was freaking out because I didn't know how I was going to pay for school. All I knew was I had heard the Lord's voice and prompting to attend the school. There was a long line of people making payments. I felt so out of place. I thought to myself, *Not only is this ridiculous, Cornelius, you are ridiculous!*

Get in line, the Holy Spirit said to me.

Lord, what am I doing here? Get me out of here.

Get in line, He said again.

While waiting in line, trying to maintain my composure and not look like an idiot, I pondered what to tell the lady at the counter. *Hi, I applied for the school. I have no money. Hi, I applied for the school. Can you loan me some money? Hi, I applied for the school. Is there by any chance I can attend it for free?*

"So, what do you want to pay for? Twenty-five dollars for the registration, four thousand dollars for the tuition, or seven thousand dollars, which includes the fees for your mission trip?" she asked.

Embarrassed and struggling for words, I replied, "Option D, none of the above." *Who does that—who shows up for school with no money to pay for it?* I asked myself.

"Cornelius, why don't you step aside, and we'll see what we can do," the lady smiled.

I don't know if she ever dealt with a student quite like me, but I was thankful for her nonjudgmental look and reassuring words.

The same day, someone paid for my registration fee, which allowed me to enroll in school. During the next few months, repeated miracles of financial provision came in. In short, all of my fees were paid, including all of my living expenses.

PRAYER OF FAITH

The Lord is my Best Friend and my Shepherd. I always have more than enough. He offers a resting place for me in his luxurious love. His tracks take me to an oasis of peace, the quiet brook of bliss. That's where he restores and revives my life. He opens before me the pathways to God's pleasure, and leads me along in his footsteps of righteousness so that I can bring honor to his name. Lord, even when your path takes me through the valley of deepest darkness, fear will never conquer me, for you already have! You remain close to me and lead me through it all the way. Your authority is my strength and my peace. The comfort of your love takes away my fear. I'll never be lonely, for you are near. You become my delicious feast even when my enemies dare to fight. You anoint me with the fragrance of your Holy Spirit; you give me all I can drink of you until my heart overflows. So why would I fear the future? For I'm being pursued only by your goodness and unfailing love. Then afterwards—when my life is through, I'll return to your glorious presence to be forever with you!

(Psalm 23 TPT)

7

SOWING IN OBEDIENCE

"Great faith isn't the ability to believe long and far into the
misty future. It's simply taking God at his word and taking
the next step."[1]
—Joni Eareckson Tada

When I was a kid, I hated greens and vegetables. My mom had to
bribe me with television time to pry my mouth open. I remember she
used to say, "Greens are good for you. You won't have pimples growing on your face if you eat them. You want the girls to like you, yes?
You want to get married when you're older, don't you?"

"Yes, Mama, feed the boy. Load up my plate!"

I didn't always listen to my mom, but I sure did then! It was a
love-hate, bittersweet relationship with greens and veggies. I knew
they were good for me, but I just couldn't stand the mushiness in my
mouth.

Perhaps that's a reflection of how some of us approach faith and
trusting God. We read the Bible, and it's all in there. We know it
behooves us to trust God for everything, but if we had it our way,
we'd rather do without it. We think that's something reserved for the
pastors and ministers, the "professional" Christians, the spiritually
elite. We'd rather stay tucked in our little corner of safety, security,
and self-sufficiency, risk-free and invulnerable. For some people, faith

and trusting God is such an abstract and inscrutable concept. We dislike the idea of the unknown, uncertainties, and unpredictability. It makes us uncomfortable, partly because we don't know how to navigate through the process of faith. Faith is the culture of the kingdom, but many of us are unaccustomed to the praxis and protocols of that culture. Faith is a spiritual concept, but it is also very practical. In the last chapter, we established how dependency is our posture in believing in God for His provision. In this chapter, my aim is to give you some tools, some "handles," to help you navigate the journey of faith.

OBEDIENCE ALWAYS PRODUCE BLESSINGS

God promises to back us up with His provision when we obey and act on what He has spoken. And, sometimes, what He tells us to do does not make sense. It takes obedience and faith to unlock His promises and provision. Think about Abraham. He and Sarah were beyond childbearing years when God called them to leave their home for an unknown country and promised Abraham that he would be a father of many nations. He stood on the word of God, and we owe our existence to him because of his obedience! Jonah, though disobedient at first, obeyed the word of the Lord and saved Nineveh from destruction. Moses obeyed the word of the Lord, and God used him to lead the Israelites out of Egypt, out of slavery, and into the Promised Land. Shadrach, Meshach, and Abednego obeyed the word of the Lord, and refused to bow down to the idol statue. God delivered them from the fiery furnace, promoting them and giving them influence. Noah obeyed the word of the Lord and built the ark when it didn't make any sense. He ended up saving his entire family.

GOD PROMISES TO BACK US UP WITH HIS PROVISION WHEN WE OBEY AND ACT ON WHAT HE HAS SPOKEN. AND, SOMETIMES, WHAT HE TELLS US TO DO DOES NOT MAKE SENSE. IT TAKES OBEDIENCE AND FAITH TO UNLOCK HIS PROMISES AND PROVISION.

On and on, story after story, we read about the courageous men and women of faith in the Bible. There's a common thread. They obeyed the word of the Lord, stood on His promises, and experienced incredible blessing, breakthrough, and provision.

In the Old Testament, there was a man Elijah, a mighty prophet used by the Lord through his obedience. He experienced radical provision as he obeyed and acted on the word of the Lord.

> *Then the word of the Lord came to him, saying, "Get away from here and turn eastward, and hide by the Brook Cherith, which flows into the Jordan. And it will be that you shall drink from the brook, and I have commanded the ravens to feed you there." So he went and did according to the word of the Lord, for he went and stayed by the Brook Cherith, which flows into the Jordan. The ravens brought him bread and meat in the morning, and bread and meat in the evening; and he drank from the brook. And it happened after a while that the brook dried up, because there had been no rain in the land. Then the word of the Lord came to him, saying, "Arise, go to Zarephath, which belongs to Sidon, and dwell there. See, I have commanded a widow there to provide for you."*   (1 Kings 17:2–9)

The New Testament records a powerful encounter between Peter and Jesus in Luke 5:1–9. Jesus was teaching by the Sea of Galilee. To avoid the crowd, He got into Simon Peter's boat. He told Peter to push out a little from the shore so that He could address the crowd and continue teaching. After teaching, Jesus told Peter to head out to fish: *"Launch out into the deep and let down your nets for a catch"* (Luke 5:4). Here is a carpenter's Son and itinerant Preacher telling a fisherman it's time to fish. The conditions weren't right for fishing. Nighttime was the best time for fishing, but it was daylight.

> *But Simon answered and said to Him, "Master, we have toiled all night and caught nothing; nevertheless at Your word I will let down the net."*   (Luke 5:5)

Peter was probably thinking to himself, *Who is this guy, telling me what to do? We've caught nothing all night. Jesus, why don't You build Your furniture and let me do my fishing. I'm the pro here.* Nevertheless, at Jesus's word, Peter complied. Peter's willingness to act probably reflected his awareness of the weight and authority in Jesus's words. After all, Peter addressed Jesus as *"Master,"* denoting someone in authority. It didn't make sense to Peter in the natural, but he recognized and chose to submit himself to the authority of Jesus's words. He went ahead and cast the net.

> *When they had done this, they caught a great number of fish, and their net was breaking. So they signaled to their partners in the other boat to come and help them. And they came and filled both the boats, so that they began to sink.… For he and all who were with him were astonished at the catch of fish which they had taken.* (Luke 5:6–7, 9)

A miracle took place. They had a net-breaking, boat-sinking catch of fish! Amid the chaos and excitement, it hit Peter. It was an unusual catch, not one accomplished through conventional fishing techniques. It was supernatural. There was power in Jesus's words. He said it, the power of God was released, and the miracle manifested right before his eyes.

Another example of someone who understood the authority and power of God's word was Mary, the mother of Jesus. When the angel Gabriel announced to her that she was going to be with a child, she questioned (just like Peter) how this would happen. It did not make any sense since she had never been with a man. God is skilled in turning impossibilities into actualities.

> *For with God nothing will be impossible. Then Mary said, "Behold the maidservant of the Lord! Let it be to me according to your word." And the angel departed from her.* (Luke 1:37–38)

Not long ago, I was teaching a Bible class one Sunday morning at Bethel Church. The night before, the Lord had spoken to a Hungarian girl who needed twelve hundred dollars for a ministry trip to Cambodia. "Go to Cornelius' class tomorrow and have him pray for you." We had never met each other before. At the end of the class, she came up to me, and explained what the Lord had told her. I told her I'd be glad to pray for her once I'd finished praying for the woman in front of me. After we prayed, I noticed the lady I had prayed for stood there the entire time, listening to our prayer.

She looked at the Hungarian girl and me and said, "While you were praying, the Holy Spirit told me to pay for her trip to Cambodia."

OBEDIENCE TO THE WORD OF THE LORD, WHETHER IT'S A PROMISE FROM SCRIPTURE OR AN INSPIRED WORD SPOKEN TO YOU FROM THE HOLY SPIRIT, ACTIVATES THE POWER AND PROVISION OF GOD.

Obedience to the word of the Lord, whether it's a promise from Scripture or an inspired word spoken to you from the Holy Spirit, activates the power and provision of God. Faith is not wishful thinking; it's standing and acting on God's word to us.

PLANT YOUR FAITH AS A SEED

Another aspect of the kingdom culture is giving and generosity. It is the nature of God to give. He gave His most precious possession, His Seed, His only Son, so that He would gain more sons and daughters in return.

An important concept of giving is seed faith. I was taught this principle as a student at Oral Roberts University. In the beginning, God said that, as long as the earth remains, there will be *"seedtime and harvest"* (Genesis 8:22). Our faith can be planted as a seed. Cause and effect is a law of the universe. Every action has a reaction or consequence.

Do not be deceived, God is not mocked; for whatever a man sows, that he will also reap.   (Galatians 6:7)

Jesus compared faith to a sown seed that has the potential to produce miraculous, "mountain moving" results. Jesus said,

> *If you have faith as a mustard seed, you will say to this mountain, "Move from here to there," and it will move; and nothing will be impossible for you.*   (Matthew 17:20)

Our faith in God is like a seed. Our faith takes on a new nature when it is released to God. Our faith itself does not have power, but when it is attached to God's miracle-working power, it produces miraculous results. When God breathes His power on our faith, it can move mountains of lack, depression, discouragement, job loss, sickness, relationship wounds, and much more. Our seeds of faith can activate the provision of God to meet our needs.

Faith is like a muscle that can be strengthened. Our confidence in God's unchanging nature can grow. God has given *"each one a measure of faith"* (Romans 12:3). Furthermore, Paul tells us that *"faith comes by hearing, and hearing by the word of God"* (Romans 10:17). Our faith comes alive when the Word of God, which is alive and powerful, is ignited inside us. Our faith is active and dynamic. We sow our seeds of faith, stand on the promises of God, and watch God release His power on our behalf.

I am a city boy. I have lived in the city most of my life. But since moving in to a new house in Redding, California, I have had to learn a few things about gardening, farming, fertilizers, soil, and seeds. We can learn a lot spiritually from the process of seeding and harvesting. A few dry patches in my backyard needed some work. I went to Lowe's and bought a pack of Scotts EZ Seed Patch and Repair. According to the instructions on the back, the three steps are:

1. PREP

Prepare the area where you want to grow grass by removing dead grass and loosening hard soil to help the tiny seedling root.

The first step to the process of faith is preparation. You have to prepare the ground so that your seed is best positioned for optimum growth. It is vital to prepare the soil of your heart by pulling out weeds and removing dead belief systems. I also got a container of Roundup to kill the roots of the weeds. What lies are you believing? Get rid of the roots of deception and lies that don't line up with the Word of God and what God says about you and your situations. In the parable of the sower in Matthew 13:3–23, the sower who receives a thirty-, sixty-, or a hundredfold harvest hears and understands the Word and will of God and does not let deception, worry, and anxiety choke up the life of the seed.

2. APPLY

Evenly apply the seeds, so the area is mostly covered, but bare ground is still visible so that the seeds contact the soil.

The next step is to apply and plant the seeds in the soil. Oral Roberts taught the three principles of seed faith. First, recognize that God is your source. Second, sow and target your seed at your need. Last, expect a miracle. Believe and declare that God is your source—not men, not Wall Street, not your ability or inability. Declare that He is a good Father who knows what, when, and how to provide. Next, target your seed at your need. The seed needs to contact the soil. What seeds are you sowing, and what are you believing God for? I plant financial seeds (seeds of time, acts of service or kindness, a smile, a generous attitude, and so forth) to meet specific needs, such as bills and expenses, good health, great relationships with friends and family, or favor at work. Believe God to work powerfully on your behalf.

3. WATER

Water deeply and thoroughly.

A good farmer not only knows how to prepare the soil and apply the seed, but he knows where he has planted and knows to keep watering the seeds. You don't sow a seed and then forget about it. Many people start off well by sowing seeds of faith, only for the seeds to die because of negligence and lack of intentionality. If you don't know where you have sown, how will you know where and when to harvest? Water your seeds by consistently speaking and declaring life to them, expecting to see them grow and, ultimately, to reap a harvest. Speak the Word of God over your needs and circumstances.

> *Death and life are in the power of the tongue, and those who love*
> *it will eat its fruit.*   (Proverbs 18:21)

The attitude and motivation with which we sow our seeds are key. I never give with an attitude or motivation of lack. Sacrifice, yes, but lack, never. I am not worse off because of my giving. I believe that God can multiply the seeds back to me in good health, favor at work, a healthy marriage, material provision, peace, joy, and other blessings that God wants to pour into my life. He knows what I need and how to bless me.

As a teenager, when the offering bucket came around, I would always be so sad to part with my money. I hated saying goodbye to the money I thought I was never going to see again. Years later, I understood that God was not taking something from me, but, in His manifold wisdom, He was getting something to me. It reoriented the way I approached giving. Now, when the offering bucket comes around, I no longer say goodbye. I say, "See you later, buddy!"

> THE SPIRIT WITH WHICH WE GIVE IS AS SIGNIFICANT
> AS THE GIFT ITSELF. WE ARE NOT TO GIVE GRUDGINGLY
> OR OUT OF COMPULSION, BUT OUT OF OUR LOVE, WORSHIP,
> AND GRATITUDE FOR ALL THAT GOD HAS DONE, IS DOING,
> AND IS GOING TO DO IN OUR LIVES.

The spirit with which we give is as significant as the gift itself. We are not to give grudgingly or out of compulsion, but out of our love, worship, and gratitude for all that God has done, is doing, and is going to do in our lives. (See 2 Corinthians 9:7.) I give generously and trust that God knows how to best provide for my needs. When we understand that God desires to multiply the seeds we have sown, it is easy to give with a cheerful heart.

It's important to point out that faith giving does not work like a cosmic jackpot machine. That's not how the kingdom works. Simon the sorcerer thought he could buy the power of God and was rebuked by Peter:

> Peter said to him, "Your money perish with you, because you thought that the gift of God could be purchased with money! You have neither part nor portion in this matter, for your heart is not right in the sight of God."   (Acts 8:20–21)

The practice of simony, which was widespread in the Catholic Church in the ninth and tenth centuries, originated from this. It was the act of buying and selling of church offices, roles, influence, and other spiritual things. We can never buy the blessings of God. We never give to get. That must not be our motive. We give simply because we love the Lord. In the kingdom, we position ourselves to receive when we give.

> Give, and it will be given to you: good measure, pressed down, shaken together, and running over will be put into your bosom. For with the same measure that you use, it will be measured back to you.   (Luke 6:38)

Jesus also said, "It is more blessed to give than to receive" (Acts 20:35). In the upside-down, paradoxical kingdom, generosity always trumps greed; self-sacrifice always trumps self-consumption; giving is always better than getting. It seems odd that giving would be better than receiving. Why did Jesus say that? What was His point? I believe that one of the primary reasons was because He can multiply only what we give, not what we receive. When the little boy gave his lunch of two fishes and five loaves of bread to the Lord, Jesus received it, blessed it, and multiplied it to feed five thousand men, besides women and children, with twelve baskets of leftovers! (See Mark 6:30–44.)

PARTNER WITH GOD WITH YOUR TITHES AND OFFERINGS

> "Bring all the tithes into the storehouse, that there may be food in My house, and try Me now in this," says the LORD of hosts, "if I

will not open for you the windows of heaven....And I will rebuke
the devourer for your sakes, so that he will not destroy the fruit
of your ground, nor shall the vine fail to bear fruit for you in the
field," says the LORD of hosts.   (Malachi 3:10–11)

Tithing is a common practice in most churches. We give God a tenth of all we have received. Offerings are gifts above and beyond the tithe. The foundational principle of our giving is this: Everything we have belongs to the Lord. One hundred percent. He owns it all. The tithe is more about who you place your dependence on than where you place the decimal point. We get to give God a small portion of all He's given to us. David understood this well when he declared these words in the assembly of the Israelites:

TITHES SHOULD BE GIVEN TO GOD FROM OUR INCREASE AND FOR OUR INCREASE. WHEN WE GIVE, WE GET TO PARTNER WITH GOD AND HIS PLANS TO BLESS AND PROVIDE FOR US.

"O LORD, the God of our ancestor Israel, may you be praised
forever and ever! Yours, O LORD, is the greatness, the power,
the glory, the victory, and the majesty. Everything in the heavens
and on earth is yours, O LORD, and this is your kingdom. We
adore you as the one who is over all things. Wealth and honor
come from you alone, for you rule over everything. Power and
might are in your hand, and at your discretion people are made
great and given strength. O our God, we thank you and praise
your glorious name! But who am I, and who are my people, that
we could give anything to you? Everything we have has come
from you, and we give you only what you first gave us!
                              (1 Chronicles 29:10–14 NLT)

I would rather have 90 percent of my money and God's blessing than 100 percent of it without His approval and blessings. Tithes should be given to God from our increase and for our increase. When we give, we get to partner with God and His plans to bless and provide for us. It's our statement of trust and faith in Him.

God provides in response to our faith. In the parable of the sower, Jesus taught that the life of a seed could be terminated by the evil one. (See Matthew 13:18.) God promised to rebuke the devourer and all that tries to sabotage the growth process and harvest. God promises to protect the seeds so that we get to reap the harvest and the blessings.

ISAAC SOWED SEEDS AND PROSPERED

In chapter 1, I discussed God's promise to bless Abraham because of the covenant He established with him. The promise to Abraham that he would be the *"heir of the world"* (Romans 4:13) was extended to his offspring Isaac and Jacob. Under His covenant, God promised these patriarchs descendants and property. Through the history of God's dealings with the Israelites, His covenant with His people was characterized by two things—His constant pursuit of relationship and restoration with His people, and His consistent provision for their needs. The plan from the beginning was not only to bless His people but to make them a blessing to others. Today, we are heirs and recipients of the promises and provision of God because of the covenant God made with Abraham.

In Genesis 26:1–11, we see that Isaac inherited the promises God made to Abraham. Isaac experienced success and prosperity because of God's blessings.

> *Then Isaac sowed in that land, and reaped in the same year a hundredfold; and the LORD blessed him. The man began to prosper, and continued prospering until he became very prosperous; for he had possessions of flocks and possessions of herds and a great number of servants.* (Genesis 26:12–14)

Here's what I want you to see. Isaac was positioned to receive the blessings of God on account of God's covenant with Abraham. Yet he did not receive the blessings of God until he sowed seeds in faith.

His act of faith in sowing released the provision that had already been promised to him. And, boy, was he blessed! To highlight the measure of blessings Isaac received, let's take a look at the passage: "*The man began to prosper, and continued prospering until he became very prosperous*" (verse 13). The word "*prosper*" was used three times. We can only imagine what it amounted to! We must be convinced that we can never out-give God.

GENEROSITY BEGETS GENEROSITY

Giving and generosity are synonymous. God takes generosity seriously because it is who He is. He demonstrated the most generous act in history by giving us His most prized possession, His one and only Son, so that we might gain. Most people think generosity is determined by the amount of a gift. Generosity is not measured by how much we give, but by how much the gift means to us. It is measured by our sacrifice. Take, for example, Bill Gates. According to Forbes, in 2016, he was the richest person in the world, with a net worth of seventy-five billion dollars.[2] Giving away two million dollars might seem like an exorbitant amount to us, but it would be spare change to him. He might not even think twice about giving that amount away.

> While Jesus was in the Temple, he watched the rich people dropping their gifts in the collection box. Then a poor widow came by and dropped in two small coins. "I tell you the truth," Jesus said, "this poor widow has given more than all the rest of them. For they have given a tiny part of their surplus, but she, poor as she is, has given everything she has."   (Luke 21:1–4 NLT)

The giving that caught Jesus's attention wasn't what the rich people gave, for they gave "*a tiny part of their surplus*," but the two coins that the poor widow gave. She gave what was most precious to her.

I remember a time in church when all I had was two dollars in my wallet. When the offering bucket came around, I felt the Holy Spirit tell me to empty my wallet. I obeyed, and the Lord took care of my expenses that entire week. Jesus never underestimated the value of giving away little things: a grain of wheat (see John 12:24), a cup of cold water (see Matthew 10:42), one talent (see Matthew 25:24), the lost coin (see Luke 15:8–10), an act of kindness done to *"the least of these"* (Matthew 25:40), and the *"five loaves and two fishes"* (Matthew 14:17).

Some of the most giving and generous people I have met are not the wealthiest people I know. There's something different I have noticed about generous people. It's not just what they have or the assets they own; it's their generous attitude.

> *Generous people plan to do what is generous, and they stand firm in their generosity.*   (Isaiah 32:8 NLT)

Generous people are magnanimous not just with finances or material things but with their words, encouragement, smiles, compassion, and acts of kindness. Generosity is not what we give; it's who we are.

THE TAYLOR GUITAR

Our giving is attached to our dependence on God. When we give what's most precious to us, we also communicate that God is most precious to us. We are saying that He alone is our Source and our dependency.

Years ago, I began to lead worship at church, and I was saving up for my dream 714ce Taylor guitar, which costs about three thousand dollars. In the meantime, I had bought a three-hundred-dollar guitar.

One day, the Lord told me to give my guitar to another worship leader. I reluctantly gave it away. Then the Lord told me to give away the money I had been saving for my dream guitar. I remember telling the Lord, "What are you doing? You took away my guitar away and now you are crushing my dream!" I caved and obeyed.

A couple of months after that, my worship pastor told me that he knew the sole distributor of Taylor guitars in Singapore. Every year, he would gather a list of names of worship leaders with certain criteria and would give away a Taylor guitar to the most deserving one. Guess who came out on top of that list and walked home with the 714ce Taylor? Yours truly!

> *The world of the generous gets larger and larger; the world of the stingy gets smaller and smaller.*   (Proverbs 11:24 MSG)

WE CAN LIMIT OUR BLESSING BY BEING TIGHTFISTED WITH OUR TIME, FINANCES, RESOURCES, ATTITUDES, AND KINDNESS. ON THE OTHER HAND, WHEN WE ARE GENEROUS, HIS PROVISION AND REWARDS HAVE NO LIMITS.

When we are generous to God, He is generous to us. It's important to give, but it is just as important to receive. Some people are so conditioned to give that they feel awkward and uncomfortable about receiving. I know people who struggle with a guilty complex about receiving or having too much. *"Freely you have received, freely give"* (Matthew 10:8). We can limit our blessing by being tightfisted with our time, finances, resources, attitudes, and kindness. On the other hand, when we are generous, His provision and rewards have no limits. Generosity begets generosity. When we give generously, God, in turn, generously provides for all our needs. Moreover, He promises to enlarge our capacity to give so that we can always be generous.

> *Remember this—a farmer who plants only a few seeds will get a small crop. But the one who plants generously will get a generous crop. You must each decide in your heart how much to give. And don't give reluctantly or in response to pressure. "For God loves a person who gives cheerfully." And God will generously provide all you need. Then you will always have everything you need and plenty left over to share with others. As the Scriptures say, "They share freely and give generously to the poor. Their good deeds will be remembered forever." For God is the one who provides seed for the farmer and then bread to eat. In the same way, he will*

provide and increase your resources and then produce a great harvest of generosity in you. Yes, you will be enriched in every way so that you can always be generous.

(2 Corinthians 9:6–11 NLT)

Our generosity can trigger the miracles of God. In 2 Kings 4:8–17, a Shunammite woman showed generous hospitality to Elisha by hosting him. Because of that, God ended her barrenness by giving her a son. In another incident, a widow in Zarephath was preparing a meal out of the little she had for her and her son. She obeyed the Word of the Lord and made a cake for Elijah. She offered what she had, and it triggered a miracle from God. She and her son had food to eat till the drought had ended! (See 1 Kings 17:13–16.)

The generous will prosper; those who refresh others will them-selves be refreshed.   (Proverbs 11:25 NLT)

MY GOD SHALL SUPPLY ALL YOUR NEEDS

My God shall supply all your need according to His riches in glory by Christ Jesus.   (Philippians 4:19)

This is one of the most well-known and quoted Scriptures in the Bible. Not only is it an astounding promise, but it reflects our core dependence on God for all our needs. It is helpful to understand the context in which Paul penned this statement. The church at Philippi is probably the best example of a missionary-supporting church in the New Testament. Paul said, "No church shared with me concerning giving and receiving but you only" (Philippians 4:15). The Philippians were a constant source of support for Paul, helping to meet his needs. Paul ended his letter to the Philippians with a statement of thanksgiving for their gifts to him:

For even in Thessalonica you sent aid once and again for my necessities. Not that I seek the gift, but I seek the fruit that abounds to your account. Indeed I have all and abound. I am full, having received from Epaphroditus the things sent from you, a sweet-smelling aroma, an acceptable sacrifice, well pleasing to God. And my God shall supply all your need according to His riches in glory by Christ Jesus. (Philippians 4:16–19)

In verse 17, Paul said, *"Not that I seek the gift, but I seek the fruit that abounds to your account."* This sentence in the Greek is full of commercial terms. Paul was not seeking personal benefits but gain for the Philippians—*"fruit that abounds to your account"* or, better understood in the Greek, "increasing profit or credit" to their account.[3] It carries the imagery of a bank account that keeps receiving compounded interest.[4] Paul views their gift to him as an investment that will pay increasing dividends with interest! Paul had set his heart on this. Even though he didn't need their gifts, he readily accepted them because he understood that their liberal giving was a seed that God could multiply on their account, and that they would ultimately receive blessings in increasing fashion!

Notice that Paul equated their giving to him as a gift to God Himself: *"The things sent from you, a sweet-smelling aroma, an acceptable sacrifice, well pleasing to God"* (Philippians 4:18). By that, Paul was implying that their gifts were of the highest quality.

> WE MUST UNDERSTAND THAT GOD IS THE ULTIMATE RECIPIENT OF EVERY SEED WE SOW INTO THE KINGDOM—NOT MEN, CHURCHES, OR MINISTRIES. HE ALONE HAS THE POWER AND CAPACITY TO MULTIPLY THE SEEDS AND BRING ABOUT A BOUNTIFUL HARVEST.

We must understand that God is the ultimate recipient of every seed we sow into the kingdom—not men, churches, or ministries. He alone has the power and capacity to multiply the seeds and bring about a bountiful harvest. Paul ends by encouraging the Philippians, that because of their generosity and sacrificial giving, they could rest in the promise that God would *"supply all your need according to his riches in glory."*

The Greek word for *"need"* was also used when Paul referred to his *"necessities"* in verse 16.[5] Paul was not referring to spiritual needs, as some would suppose, but to material and physical needs. Not only will God provide our material and physical needs, but He will do so in a glorious manner, on a scale worthy of His wealth, in accordance with His marvelous riches! His wealth is limitless; it cannot be exhausted, even with all our needs combined. The glorious immensity of God's riches and resources allows no room for a "lack" mind-set.

We can trust God right now to supply all our needs for today. If our needs are greater tomorrow, His supply will be greater also. He alone is our source, and we can trust in His abundance and ability to take care of us when we choose to sow liberally into the kingdom in worship and love for Him. That's the beauty of His grace, not that we can earn His blessings with our giving, but that He freely gives out of His riches in response to our sacrificial worship, generosity, and faith.

PRAYER OF FAITH

Lord, thank You that You are the generous Father. I declare that I will always have everything I need and more so that I can always share with others. I am a cheerful giver. I know that, when I give, it will be given back to me. A good measure, pressed down, shaken together, and running over will be poured into my lap. I know that, with the measure I give, it will be given back to me. I will be rewarded because I sow in obedience. May my life be a reflection of Your generosity. Amen!

8

THE ACTS OF FAITH

"Faith is the bucket of power lowered by the rope of
prayer into the well of God's abundance.
What we bring up depends upon what we let down.
We have every encouragement to use a big bucket."[1]
—Virginia Whitman

Our faith is active. Something happens when we declare the nature
of God and His promises. Our words have creative power. Faith
recognizes God's power to create. The universe was not created in a
vacuum. It came into existence because God uttered a performative
and dynamic word.

> *By faith we understand that the worlds were framed by the word
> of God, so that the things which are seen were not made of things
> which are visible.* (Hebrews 11:3)

He is the God who *"calls those things which did not exist as though
they did"* (Romans 4:17). Faith pulls on heaven's resources by speaking out and declaring God's will until it has manifested in the natural.
Faith is more than self-confession or positive thinking. God works in
accordance with His will, not our wishes. We understand His will
when we understand His heart revealed through His Word. When
we do that, we have every confidence to stand on His promises, and
believe and declare them by faith until we see their manifestation.

119

Now this is the confidence that we have in Him, that if we ask anything according to His will, He hears us. And if we know that He hears us, whatever we ask, we know that we have the petitions that we have asked of Him.   (1 John 5:14–15)

Our tongue is a weapon of faith, capable of shifting atmospheres and moving mountains of impossibilities. The tongue has the power to speak life or death. (See Proverbs 18:21.)

Now in the morning, as they passed by, they saw the fig tree dried up from the roots. And Peter, remembering, said to Him, "Rabbi, look! The fig tree which You cursed has withered away." So Jesus answered and said to them, "Have faith in God. For assuredly, I say to you, whoever says to this mountain, 'Be removed and be cast into the sea,' and does not doubt in his heart, but believes that those things he says will be done, he will have whatever he says. Therefore I say to you, whatever things you ask when you pray, believe that you receive them, and you will have them.
(Mark 11:20–24)

We can understand this passage in the context of prayer. It is interesting that Jesus used a fig tree to teach His disciples to have faith in God. The power of Jesus's words caused the fig tree to wither within a day. Jesus never commanded or commissioned His disciples to do anything without first showing them how to do it. He showed them that those who put their faith in God could activate His miraculous power by speaking directly to impossible situations. God moves "mountains" through those who have become habituated to a life of trust and faith in God.

A PERSON WITH FAITH BELIEVES ENOUGH TO ASK AND DECLARE. OUR FAITH IN GOD'S CHARACTER AND PROMISES AND OUR COMMITMENT TO DO HIS WILL SHOULD GIVE US THE CONFIDENCE THAT WHATEVER WE ASK WILL HAPPEN.

Faith is the opposite of doubt and fear. It is an intentional decision to trust in Jesus despite the contrary, and to expect from Him
what only He can provide. A person with faith believes enough to ask
and declare. Our faith in God's character and promises and our commitment to do His will should give us the confidence that whatever
we ask will happen. There is a correlation between prayer and faith,
and faith and speaking. A prayer of faith trusts in God's immovable
steadfastness and confidently declares His Word and promises.

You will also declare a thing, and it will be established for you; so
light will shine on your ways.   (Job 22:28)

We need to keep watering our seeds and the things we are believing God for by speaking faith and life to them. Whatever you believe,
you have to speak it. The quality of your seed is determined by your
confession. When we declare something, we are agreeing with it.
When I look in the mirror in the morning and declare, "You are the
hottest and spiciest Asian alive," I am agreeing with that statement,
even though it requires a massive amount of faith every time I say it!
The point is, our words follow our faith and belief.

Since we have the same spirit of faith, according to what is writ-
ten, "I believed and therefore I spoke," we also believe and there-
fore speak.   (2 Corinthians 4:13)

"ELI, I AM COMING FOR YOU!"

When I was sixteen, a missionary gave me a prophetic word,
saying, "One day, you are going to go to ORU."

End of conversation. I didn't know what or where ORU was. I
later found out it was Oral Roberts University. I shelved it and went
on with my life. Thirteen years later, I was studying at a seminary in
London, England, and the Holy Spirit spoke to me, "Now is the time
to go to ORU!"

It made absolutely no sense. I had started the program at the
seminary a few months earlier. Moreover, I didn't have the money or

the resources to make the transition. However, the word of the Lord wouldn't let me go. The conviction grew stronger and stronger. I had to bring all my excuses, reasoning, fears, and doubts before the Lord.

Then the spirit of faith kicked in. I went to the ORU website, downloaded and printed out the college mascot, Eli, the golden eagle. I pinned it to the corkboard above my study table. Multiple times a day for two months, I would look squarely at Eli and declare, "Eli, the Lord has spoken. I am coming for you!"

In the fall of that same year, I set foot on the campus of Oral Roberts University as a student.

FAITH ACTIVATES HEAVEN'S REALITY

Hebrews 11 is often referred to as the "hall of faith." Listed in this chapter are men and women who have demonstrated great faith and performed mighty exploits in God. Hebrews 11:1 reveals the essence of faith:

> Now faith is the substance of things hoped for, the evidence of things not seen.

Here, faith is oriented to things not yet present or visible. The *Amplified Bible* puts it this way:

> Now faith is the assurance (title deed, confirmation) of things hoped for (divinely guaranteed), and the evidence of things not seen [the conviction of their reality—faith comprehends as fact what cannot be experienced by the physical senses].

The word *"assurance"* is translated from the Greek word *hypostasis*, which communicates the idea of substance, confidence, a "title deed," "guarantee," or "proof."[2] It is to be understood as a firm, solid confidence or calm courage concerning the things hoped for. The second half of the verse carries a parallel meaning, *"the evidence of things not seen."* The Greek word used for *"evidence"* here is *elenchos*, meaning conviction, "proof," or "demonstration."[3] Theologian Phillip Hughes defines it as:

It is not a static emotion of complacency but something lively and active, not just an immovable dogmatism but of a vital certainty which impels the believer to stretch out his hand, as it were, and lay hold of those realities on which his hope is fixed and which, though unseen, are already his in Christ.[4]

I like that. Faith is a compelling force that motivates and inspires us to stretch out our hands, reach out to heaven, and lay hold of those realities—His promises and will over our lives—which, though unseen, are already ours in Christ! That's powerful! Paul understood this well. That's why he penned these words:

We do not look at the things which are seen, but at the things which are not seen. For the things which are seen are temporary, but the things which are not seen are eternal.
(2 Corinthians 4:18)

For we walk by faith, not by sight.   (2 Corinthians 5:7)

Faith is a radical concept. It convicts us that whatever God has promised is real; we count on it as a certainty. For example, you have faith that Christ is in heaven even though you have never seen Him there. In addition, you believe that the chair you are sitting on is going to hold you up even though you have no idea how it was made. Your faith conditioned you to its reality. That's the process and result of faith—we are conditioned to believe in a greater reality, heaven's reality, which is often contrary to what is seen, felt, or experienced in the natural.

FAITH IS A KEY THAT UNLOCKS THE RESOURCES OF HEAVEN, WITH WHICH WE ACCESS ALL OUR NEEDS AND PROVISION FROM GOD.

That is why Jesus and Paul could make bold statements as *"Seek first the kingdom of God…, and all these things shall be added to you"* (Matthew 6:33), and *"My God shall supply all your need according to His riches in glory by Christ Jesus"* (Philippians 4:19). To them, faith in God's provision was a fact, not just a great idea. They believed in the reality before its manifestation. Faith is a key that unlocks the resources of heaven, with which we access all our needs and provision from God. With such faith, the great saints of old received divine approval and commendation, and their example has been placed on permanent record to inspire generations to come. (See Hebrews 11:2.) This is the kind of faith that pleases God. (See Hebrews 11:6.)

An excellent example of a great man whose faith pleased God was Abraham. He believed in a God *"who gives life to the dead and calls those things which do not exist as though they did"* (Romans 4:17). Scripture says,

> [Abraham], *contrary to hope, in hope believed, so that he became the father of many nations, according to what was spoken.... And not being weak in faith, he did not consider his own body, already dead (since he was about a hundred years old), and the deadness of Sarah's womb. He did not waver at the promise of God through unbelief, but was strengthened in faith, giving glory to God, and being fully convinced that what He had promised He was also able to perform.* (Romans 4:18–21)

> *By faith Abraham obeyed when he was called to go out to the place which he would receive as an inheritance. And he went out, not knowing where he was going....By faith Sarah herself also received strength to conceive seed, and she bore a child when she was past the age, because she judged Him faithful who had promised.* (Hebrews 11:8, 11)

Abraham was seventy-five and Sarah sixty-five when the Lord promised him that he would be a father of many nations. (See Genesis 12:1–4.) Evidently, they both were beyond childbearing years. Their bodies didn't look or function as they had before. In the natural, it was an impossibility.

You see, faith puts a demand on the miracle-working power of God. Abraham and Sarah needed to look beyond the natural, and position themselves in faith for supernatural intervention.

The miracle of Isaac wasn't delivered until twenty-five years later. However, the answer to the promise, the manifestation of the miracle that was later to come, was set in motion the very moment Abraham acted on his faith and departed from Haran. His act of faith and obedience activated the power of God.

Our obedience and trust in God releases the dynamic activity and provision of heaven way before its manifestation. Arthur Peake, an English Bible scholar, put it succinctly:

> Faith thus has a power of realisation, by which the invisible becomes visible and the future becomes present. While hope is the confident anticipation of a future regarded as future, faith appropriates that future as an experience of the present.[5]

Mark 11:24 says, "*Therefore I tell you, whatever you ask for in prayer, believe that you have received it, and it will be yours*" (NIV). The Greek word translated "*received*" here is in the aorist tense, implying that we should believe that what we ask for in prayer (in accordance with His will) is not only happening but that we have already received it.[6]

THE NINETEEN MILES MIRACLE

One of my favorite faith narratives is in Joshua 3, where we read about Joshua leading the Israelites across the river Jordan.

> *It shall come to pass, as soon as the soles of the feet of the priests who bear the ark of the LORD, the Lord of all the earth, shall rest in the waters of the Jordan, that the waters of the Jordan shall be cut off, the waters that come down from upstream, and they shall stand as a heap. So it was, when the people set out from their camp to cross over the Jordan, with the priests bearing the ark of the covenant before the people, and as those who bore the ark came to the Jordan, and the feet of the priests who bore the ark dipped in the edge of the water (for the Jordan overflows all its banks during the whole time of harvest), that the waters which*

*came down from upstream stood still, and rose in a heap very
far away at Adam, the city that is beside Zaretan. So the waters
that went down into the Sea of the Arabah, the Salt Sea, failed,
and were cut off; and the people crossed over opposite Jericho.
Then the priests who bore the ark of the covenant of the* Lord
*stood firm on dry ground in the midst of the Jordan; and all
Israel crossed over on dry ground, until all the people had crossed
completely over the Jordan.*   (Joshua 3:13–17)

When the priests obeyed the word of the Lord, "*the waters which
came down from upstream stood still, and rose in a heap very far away at
Adam*" (verse 16). Adam was located about nineteen miles upstream.
Now, you couldn't see squat for nineteen miles. It's too far of a distance. Even though the whole nation of Israel couldn't see it in the
natural, at the very moment the priests dipped their toes into the
river, the power of God was released nineteen miles away! The waters
kept rising up until the they were cut off, and the Israelites witnessed
the miracle right before their eyes! The moment faith is activated,
the miracle working power of God is set into motion, and it gains
momentum until it fully manifests in due time!

FLYING BLIND

My good friend, Dr. Jennifer Miskov, has an inspiring testimony
about relying on God's voice, navigating through doubts and fear,
stepping out in faith, and watching God orchestrate a miracle of provision on her behalf. Here is her story:

"Having no money to my name, I was determined to make it to
a friend's wedding in England, even if that meant packing my bags,
and showing up at the airport without a ticket. For many months, I'd
had it in my heart to be there for her wedding. In the natural, it was
impossible for me to make the trip because I had recently finished a
work project, and was still searching for my next paid assignment.
Even though I was not able to come up with the money before the
wedding, I still felt strongly that I was supposed to be there. I had
even RSVPed months before by faith.

"On Monday, May 26, I sent out a newsletter informing my friends that I would be in England later that week. I felt I needed to do this as a declaration of faith, believing that what I felt God was doing would come to pass in His miraculous way. I had arranged to start my journey toward the airport on Tuesday. I struggled with doubt and fear just before heading out. With only a tank full of gas in my car and my bags packed, I set off for the airport with no money for the air ticket. I have noticed that, in the Bible, many miracles happen 'on the way' when people responded in faith. I believed that the same would happen for me. I spent the night in Oakland, California, at the Home of Peace, a healing home founded by Carrie Judd Montgomery. There, I ran into a friend who gave me a check for five hundred dollars toward the air ticket! I thanked God that the miracle was already happening. I still needed more than a thousand dollars, though.

"When I arrived at San Francisco International Airport the next day, I felt led to get in line at the United Airlines counter. I handed the man my passport as if I had a seat on the flight. I wondered if, by some miracle, a ticket would appear. Well, he couldn't find it. My name wasn't in the system. Having never been on a standby flight, I asked him about it, and he asked me who my "buddy" was. I told him Jesus, because I had no idea what he was talking about, and Jesus was my only hope. He proceeded to explain to me that, to fly standby, I needed to have a friend who worked for United Airlines. There were no open doors there, but I felt God in that interaction. After many other attempts of stepping out in faith to see if any other airlines would open up with no success, doubt, discouragement, and sadness set into my heart. If it were not for my friends with me, who still had hope, I would have given up.

"My friends asked me if I knew anyone who worked for an airline. A thought came to my mind to message my friend Cristina who lived in Colorado. I knew she worked for an airline, but I didn't know which one. She called me and told me that she worked for another airline that also did buddy passes even though she had never done one before. Within moments, she asked me for my passport details as I hurried toward the airline counter. I made it to the kiosk, and proceeded to type in my information. And, what do you know? My name appeared on the computer screen, and then out popped a ticket from San Francisco to London! Praise God! Cristina ended up getting my ticket for only $578, a third of the price of a regular ticket! Not only that, just before going through customs, a friend who had to drop off his car at the airport found me, walked over to an ATM, and gave me $200!

"I share this testimony with you, not that you will show up at airports without a ticket when you want to travel, but to encourage you to stay close to Jesus and the body of Christ, and to follow your heart, step out in faith, and watch God orchestrate His miracle on your behalf!"

FAITH CONTENDS

We live in a society where we want everything to happen on demand. Someone once said, "We live in a microwave world, but we serve a crockpot God." It sure feels like it sometimes. I don't mind the crockpot cooking, as long as it tastes good when it's done cooking! Thank God that He promised it will always turn out good in the end. (See Romans 8:28.) Our God is Lord and sovereign over all things, including time.

> FATE IS A PASSIVE ACCEPTANCE OF NATURE'S CIRCUMSTANCES.
> FAITH, ON THE CONTRARY, IS THE ACTIVE ANTICIPATION
> OF HEAVEN'S INTERVENTION. FAITH, NOT FATE,
> IS A KINGDOM PARADIGM.

God can do whatever He wants, whenever He wants, however He wants. His thoughts and ways are higher than ours. (See Isaiah 55:8.) We will save ourselves much headache and frustration if we learn to quickly acknowledge and embrace His lordship over our lives, including His perfect timing. The attitude with which we do that is crucial. We don't drag ourselves around, singing, "*Que será,*

será" (whatever will be, will be). We don't resign ourselves to fate. Fate is a passive acceptance of nature's circumstances. Faith, on the contrary, is the active anticipation of heaven's intervention. Faith, not fate, is a kingdom paradigm.

What do we do while we wait for God's breakthrough and provision for our lives? We develop tenacity and learn to contend. We become more resolute in our faith. Sometimes, the breakthrough and provision we are asking for are instantaneous; other times, it takes longer, but faith never compromises the belief in God's timing and wisdom. We will talk more about the timing of God in the next chapter.

SILENCE THE CHATTERBOX WITH YOUR FAITH

The devil will try to sabotage our faith by sowing lies into our minds. If he can corrupt our minds with his crafty and deceptive schemes, he can nullify our faith. The battle is in the mind. That's why it is critical that we *be transformed by the renewing of [our] mind, that [we] may prove what is that good and acceptable and perfect will of God*" (Romans 12:2). We need to continually renew our minds and feed our spirit with the Word and promises of God. When we stand on His promises, they will be tested. It's an inevitable part of the faith process. The Word of the Lord tested Joseph concerning the dream that God had given him.

> *Until the time that his word came to pass, the word of the* LORD *tested him.* (Psalm 105:19)

The devil's stereotypical modus operandi in tempting God's people is always to: (1) test the resolve of their trust and faith in God's Word; (2) unsettle their identity in Him; and (3) assassinate the character of God.

"Eve, did God really say you can't eat of every tree in the garden?"

"Jesus, are you really the Son of God? If you are the Son of God…"

"Joseph, did God really speak to you in that dream? Who do you think you are that your family will bow to you?"

"Moses, do you really think you are going to deliver Israel? Look at you, you can't even speak!"

"Abraham and Sarah, you think God's going to give you a baby? Have you looked at your bodies lately?"

"David, who told you you're going to be a king? You're just a shepherd boy. And you think you're going to slay Goliath? You're a midget. You're a joke."

Every giant of faith in the Bible has had their dreams and promises of provision tested. None of us are exempt. It goes without saying that the enemy does not want us to be blessed.

"Did God really say He's going to provide for your every need?

"Did God really promise you [fill in the blank]?"

"Are you sure He's going to keep His Word?"

"If God really cares for you, He would have provided for you by now. Your faith didn't work."

"Who do you think you are? You're a sinner. Look at you—you are sorry and pitiful."

The chatterbox is real and loud, but God has given us His Word to combat the barrage of the enemy's lies. His Word ignites faith to extinguish the lies.

Paul talks about the shield of faith in the armor of God *"with which you will be able to quench all the fiery darts of the wicked one"* (Ephesians 6:16). Here, Paul was referring to the large shield Roman infantry used to protect their entire body. Such shields were four feet tall and two and a half feet wide, and were constructed using leather stretched over wood, reinforced with metal at the top and bottom. The animal skins that covered the shields would extinguish the incendiary arrows, preventing the wood from catching fire. Moreover, before battle, the soldiers would immerse the shields in water, soaking the leather cover and canvas beneath to further aid in extinguishing the burning arrows. Remarkably, the Word of God is also referred to as water. (See Ephesians 5:26.)

In this context, faith is confident trust in God's power to protect the whole person. Faith grabs hold of God's resources in the midst of demonic onslaught, and produces confident trust in God's ability to utterly annihilate the works of darkness aimed at you! When we put our faith in God's power and His Word, it not only stops the fiery weapons of attack, but it actually extinguishes them, rendering them useless!

> *For the weapons of our warfare are not carnal but mighty in God for pulling down strongholds, casting down arguments and every high thing that exalts itself against the knowledge of God, bringing every thought into captivity to the obedience of Christ.*
> (2 Corinthians 10:4–5)

The Word of God is our trump card. It is also the sword of the Spirit with which we slay and disempower the enemy's lies and nullify his assignments. Our mind, thoughts, and imaginations are a battleground. We can't afford to let the enemy fortify his strongholds in these areas. Resistance from the enemy is to be expected. His sole assignment is to steal, kill, and destroy the saints of God. (See John 10:10.) It infuriates him that the integrity of God's character and His goodness remain intact, and that the saints of God are being blessed.

IN CONTENDING FOR THE PROMISES AND PROVISION OF GOD IN THE WAITING, WE HAVE TO STRENGTHEN OUR FAITH BY CONSISTENTLY CONFESSING AND DECLARING THE TRUTH OF GOD'S WORD, AND THE PROMISES HE HAS SPOKEN TO US.

One of the key lessons I have learned over the years is to shorten my "recovery time" when the enemy launches an attack. It used to take me a long time to recover, but now it takes much less, if any at all. I have learned to respond and condition my mind to the truth of God's Word, and quickly reject the lies of the enemy. Someone once said, "You can't stop a bird from flying over your head, but you can stop it from nesting." Refuse to let the lies of the enemy fester in your head. In contending for the promises and provision of God in the waiting, we have to strengthen our faith by consistently confessing and declaring the truth of God's Word, and the promises He has spoken to us.

CELEBRATION FUELS THE ATMOSPHERE OF FAITH

One of my wife's and my favorite things to do is celebrate. We intentionally look for reasons to celebrate. We celebrate small things like the end of a work week, the victory of my favorite soccer team (Manchester United), success in keeping to our diet or workout goals for the week, and obedient behavior from our cat. And, of course, we find great joy and fulfillment in celebrating significant events like birthdays, anniversaries, graduations, or buying a new house. Let me tell you what that does for us. It not only keeps the fun in our marriage, but it also fuels the atmosphere of faith, and keeps us expectant of all the promises of God that we are believing for. Celebration is an attitude that acknowledges and anticipates God's power to provide.

King David was acquainted with the spirit of celebration. That man knew how to dance and celebrate, even if that meant looking like a lunatic and being misunderstood. He could care less about what people thought. He cared only about the approval of the One who was deserving and worthy of his extravagant, over-the-top celebration. He knew that the presence of God demanded his uninhibited and unbridled praise and celebration.

> *Now it was told King David, saying, "The LORD has blessed the house of Obed-Edom and all that belongs to him, because of the ark of God." So David went and brought up the ark of God from the house of Obed-Edom to the City of David with gladness....Then David danced before the LORD with all his might; and David was wearing a linen ephod. So David and all the house of Israel brought up the ark of the LORD with shouting and with the sound of the trumpet. Now as the ark of the LORD came into the City of David, Michal, Saul's daughter, looked*

through a window and saw King David leaping and whirling before the LORD; and she despised him in her heart.

(2 Samuel 6:12, 14–16)

David honored and revered the presence of God. He knew that the ark of God, which represented the presence of God, brought the blessings of God. The goodness of God is synonymous with the presence of God. You can't separate one from the other. In His presence, we find goodness, kindness, peace, and fullness of joy. (See Psalm 16:11.) David celebrated the presence, goodness, and promises of God. He danced (and it wasn't a cute little two-step). It was literally a "spinning around," a rejoicing that was typical in the celebration of victories at that time. However, such behavior was common only among womenfolk, and certainly not the king. But it didn't stop David. He celebrated because He knew who His God was. When Michal, his wife, showed contempt and questioned what seemed to her to be offensive behavior, David was unapologetic about his exuberant joy.

Then David returned to bless his household. And Michal the daughter of Saul came out to meet David, and said, "How glorious was the king of Israel today, uncovering himself today in the eyes of the maids of his servants, as one of the base fellows shamelessly uncovers himself!" So David said to Michal, "It was before the LORD, who chose me instead of your father and all his house, to appoint me ruler over the people of the LORD, over Israel. Therefore I will play music before the LORD. And I will be even more undignified than this, and will be humble in my own sight....Therefore Michal the daughter of Saul had no children to the day of her death.

(2 Samuel 6:20–23)

Michal didn't share her husband's honor, reverence, and enthusiasm for the presence of God. She was stuck in her pride, just like her dad, Saul. Sadly, it resulted in her barrenness. There is good reason to believe that, had Michal celebrated the presence of the Lord, she would not have been barren. There's something about celebrating the presence of God that gives birth to His promises in our lives.

THE DREAM HOUSE

My wife, Tiffany, and I have made it a habit to celebrate by faith before we see the fruition of God's promises and provision. We believe that doing so activates the power of God and pulls from heaven's resources. In early 2016, we decided to buy a house in Redding, California, where we currently reside. We were confident that we had heard from the Lord that it was the right time to purchase. We found our dream house. We put in an offer, and the process was moving along smoothly until we hit a snag, and it looked like the deal was falling through.

I told Tiffany, "Babe, if we believe this is God's house for us, nothing can take that from us. Let's celebrate that God's going to work it out!"

That evening, we decided to go to a fancy restaurant in that neighborhood. As we said grace, we prayed, "Father, we believe that you have spoken to us concerning this house. By faith, we trust that You will work the details out. Now, we just celebrate Your goodness and provision in advance. We announce our arrival into the neighborhood! The neighborhood welcomes us! It will be better off because we are here!"

Two months later, we moved in to our dream house!

"Sing, O barren, you who have not borne! Break forth into singing, and cry aloud, you who have not labored with child! For more are the children of the desolate than the children of the married woman," says the LORD.   (Isaiah 54:1)

YOU CANNOT CELEBRATE THE GOODNESS OF GOD WITHOUT BEING GRATEFUL AND THANKFUL. THANK HIM IN ADVANCE. PRAISE HIM FOR THE PROVISION THAT IS COMING YOUR WAY. WORSHIP HIM IN THE WAITING.

Faith sings and celebrates the breakthroughs and promises of God from far off all the way to their manifestation. You cannot celebrate the goodness of God without being grateful and thankful. Thank Him in advance. Praise Him for the provision that is coming your way. Worship Him in the waiting. *"Worship the LORD your God, and his blessing will be on your food and water"* (Exodus 23:25 NIV). Praise, worship, and celebration position you for great provision. The antithesis of celebration and gratitude is murmuring and complaining. They have the capacity to sabotage your faith. Thank Him even when the circumstances look bleak. You don't have to feel great to be grateful. The significance of thanksgiving is more than the feeling of gratitude; it is the covenantal agreement concerning who God is and what He can do on your behalf.

PRAYER OF FAITH

Declare with me:

I have the Spirit of faith. I will lay hold of God's Word, His promises, and His will over my life. I know the will of God, and I pray according to His will. My tongue is a weapon of faith. With it, I shift atmospheres, move mountains, and silence the lies of the enemy. I will celebrate Your presence, goodness, kindness, and generosity toward me. I will call those things which did not exist as though they did, for I walk by faith and not by sight. With God, all things are possible! Amen!

9

SAY YES TO HIS TIMING

"To everything there is a season,
a time for every purpose under heaven."
—Ecclesiastes 3:1

One of the hardest things to do is wait. We hate to wait in line at the grocery store, in traffic, at restaurants, for Christmas presents, and for the food in the microwave. God seems to value timing more than we do. Few of us have conditioned ourselves to embrace His sovereign timing with wholehearted surrender. But those who have been trained by it will experience God's peace and contentment in the waiting. Timing is so crucial in God's orientation of things that even His name reflects it. He is the Alpha and Omega, the first and the last. He has full knowledge of what is to happen, when it should happen, and how it should happen. A set time is attached to every single one of God's plans, purposes, and promises. His foreknowledge and wisdom are beyond our comprehension.

> *For Sarah conceived and bore Abraham a son in his old age, at the set time of which God had spoken to him.* (Genesis 21:2)

> *Is anything too hard for the LORD? At the appointed time I will return to you, according to the time of life, and Sarah shall have a son.* (Genesis 18:14)

If anyone had to learn to trust in God's timing for His provision, it was Abraham (and Sarah). They were the champions of faith. They had to wait twenty-five years before the promised Isaac was born. I can imagine them winding down every evening, in the cool of the Mesopotamian desert, staring at the constellations of stars in the night sky, and wondering how their descendants would be as numerous as that. I can imagine them praying together before going to bed each night: "Lord, we've lost count of how many times we have prayed and declared, but tonight we do it one more time. Lord, you have spoken to us about having a child. You are trustworthy and faithful to Your promises. We embrace Your perfect timing. Thank You, Lord."

I imagine they prayed, they declared, they trusted, they doubted, they cried, they struggled, they refused to quit, they chose to believe, they kept saying yes to the promise. They waited for twenty-five years—9,125 nights.

> GOD IS TOO WISE AND LOVING TO ALLOW THE WAITING SEASON TO BE IN VAIN. GOD WILL MAKE OUR WAITING SEASON MEANINGFUL AND PURPOSEFUL WHEN WE TRUST HIM.

One of the most powerful heart postures of prayer is submitting oneself to His timing. Take the focus off the things you are praying for and say, "Lord, I trust in your perfect timing." The Lord knows all things. In His perfect timing, He will give and provide for you the very things that are attached to that timing. The Bible is full of stories of people who waited for God's promises to come to pass. Noah waited a long time for the rain to come after he started building the ark. God told Moses he would lead the Israelites out of slavery, but then made him wait in the desert for forty years. David was anointed when he was fifteen years old, but he didn't start to reign over Israel until he was thirty. Joseph was sold into slavery by his brothers at the age of seventeen. He had to endure thirteen years of trials and challenges before God raised him up to be second-in-command in Egypt at thirty years old. Mary and Martha were exasperated because Jesus took so long to come and heal Lazarus. Jesus Himself waited till He was thirty before beginning His ministry. You get the picture. God seems to be at ease with waiting.

From our perspective, waiting in obscurity is unsettling and frustrating. We have everything planned, and we want God to move according to our time frame. But God rarely does things according to our time frame. If we aren't careful, we can end up thinking that God is uncaring, inattentive, absentminded, or mad at us. It can easily rob us of our peace and joy. I have realized that waiting is an inevitable part of life. I have also learned that God is intentional about time and waiting. There is a God-intended purpose behind every waiting season because *"all things work together for good"* (Romans 8:28). God is too wise and loving to allow the waiting season to be in vain. God will make our waiting season meaningful and purposeful when we trust Him.

WAITING DEVELOPS PATIENCE AND ENDURANCE

Patience is such a virtue in kingdom living that it is included as one of the fruits of the Spirit. It is also one of the least welcomed fruits. Patience is one of those things that you know is good for you, but you'd rather do without. We don't readily appreciate or acknowledge its value or experience its fruit. Patience is so highly regarded by God that, if we are not careful, we can forfeit the blessings of God by being impatient, presumptuous, and taking things into our own hands. Look at Saul. His impatience resulted in losing his position as ruler over the kingdom of Israel. (See 1 Samuel 13:8–14.) Our impatience is reflective of our lack of trust in God.

Faith works together with patience. It should be the hallmark of every believer who desires to walk in the blessings of God. Paul instructs us to *"imitate those who through faith and patience inherit the promises"* (Hebrews 6:12). It is not enough to have faith. We have to have patience and endurance, dogged determination, a "refusing to let go and give up" attitude. Abraham excelled in faith; he also excelled in patience and endurance. He stuck it out and was blessed and approved by God.

> When God made his promise to Abraham, he backed it to the hilt, putting his own reputation on the line. He said, "I promise that I'll bless you with everything I have—bless and bless and bless!" Abraham stuck it out and got everything that had been promised to him. (Hebrews 6:14 MSG)

> So let's not allow ourselves to get fatigued doing good. At the right time we will harvest a good crop if we don't give up, or quit. (Galatians 6:9 MSG)

> These all wait for You, that You may give them their food in due season. (Psalm 104:27)

Jacob is another fine example of someone who persevered in patience and was rewarded beautifully (pun intended). Jacob worked seven years for Laban for the promise of beautiful Rachel in marriage. On his wedding night, Laban sneaked Leah (who was not attractive) into the wedding bed in place of Rachel. It is very unfortunate that ancient lamps provided little light. Alas, Jacob consummated the marriage with Leah, not Rachel. This could have been an episode of the *Desperate Housewives of Ancient Harran*! I would not wish this wedding night shenanigans upon anyone. I am thankful for incandescent, bright white, 100,000 lumen bulbs—that's all I'm saying! As the story goes, Jacob said yes to Laban, and agreed to work for him for another seven years for Rachel. Fourteen years of sacrificial labor, enduring courtship, and unrelenting love for the hand of the woman of his dreams. Something in this story stands out to me—Jacob's love for Rachel made the waiting season seem like a breeze. He got to behold Rachel's beauty all that time.

> So Jacob served seven years for Rachel, and they seemed only a few days to him because of the love he had for her. (Genesis 29:20)

Waiting for a promise or provision to come to pass is undeniably stretching and uncomfortable. But could setting our love and affection on the Lover of our souls make our seasons of waiting fleeting, purposeful, delightful, and sweet? He's worth the wait. It's going to be good. Be encouraged.

A PROPHETIC INSIGHT

> So Jacob agreed to work seven more years. A week after Jacob had married Leah, Laban gave him Rachel, too.... So Jacob slept with Rachel, too, and he loved her much more than Leah. He then stayed and worked for Laban the additional seven years.
> (Genesis 29:28, 30 NLT)

It is worthy to note that when Jacob said yes to Laban, agreeing to work another seven years, Laban gave Rachel to Jacob in marriage in accelerated time—in seven days. He didn't have to wait the whole seven years.

Let me speak prophetically here. I believe our "yes" activates the provision and promises of God. I believe that heaven eagerly awaits the yes of the saints of God. I believe that God's assignments are lined up in heaven, ready to be discharged when God's people answer the call. I believe that our yes is so powerful that it arrests the attention of the hosts of heaven. I imagine heaven responding, "The ones who say yes to God are the ones God can use in the kingdom. Heaven's resources belong to the ones who have obeyed heaven's call for kingdom assignments. The provision of heaven is released to them to execute and establish the purposes of God on the earth."

THAT'S THE ESSENCE OF FAITH. FAITH SAYS YES TO GOD'S WILL AND WAITS IN EXPECTANCY FOR THE MANIFESTATION OF HIS PROVISION AND PROMISES.

Jacob's yes accelerated the fulfillment of a promise. I believe that, when we posture our hearts in wholehearted surrender and obedience, saying yes to His will and timing, at that moment, we activate the resources of heaven concerning that which heaven has called us to. That's the essence of faith. Faith says yes to God's will and waits in expectancy for the manifestation of His provision and promises.

"I WON'T LET YOU GO UNLESS YOU BLESS ME"

Later in Jacob's life, we read of one of the most powerful and mysterious narratives in the Bible. He wrestled with the angel of the Lord for his blessing.

> *Then Jacob was left alone; and a Man wrestled with him until the breaking of day. Now when He saw that He did not prevail against him, He touched the socket of his hip; and the socket of Jacob's hip was out of joint as He wrestled with him. And He said, "Let Me go, for the day breaks." But he said, "I will not let You go unless You bless me!" So He said to him, "What is your name?" He said, "Jacob." And He said, "Your name shall no longer be called Jacob, but Israel; for you have struggled with God and with men, and have prevailed."* (Genesis 32:24–28)

I have always wondered where and how Jacob found the audacity, strength, and tenacity to wrestle with an angel for his blessing. Jacob was a fighter. I like to imagine that etched at the back of his mind, he remembered how he had fought and endured fourteen years for his promised bride. He recalled how he had struggled and prevailed. Jacob's patient endurance and perseverance had developed in him a tenacity that now positioned and equipped him to contend not just with man but with God for his blessing. He knew that God had willed to bless him (see Genesis 32:12), and he would not settle for anything less than his inheritance (see Genesis 32:26). His contending tenacity caused him to prevail again. Our endurance and perseverance develop greater strength and tenacity in us to believe God for greater things. God is always enlarging our capacity so that we can contain and experience more of His blessings and, in turn, be a greater blessing to others.

God responded to Jacob's unwavering attitude and strength by changing his name from Jacob (deceiver, supplanter) to Israel (God-wrestler, God-will-prevail).

> *Your name shall no longer be called Jacob, but Israel; for you*
> *have struggled with God and with men, and have prevailed.*
> (Genesis 32:28)

Because Jacob persisted and did not give up, he was blessed with a new identity; he went from being mediocre to blessed. When you contend in faith and endurance and choose to believe in God's utmost best for your life, God will change your identity from lack, sick, depressed, and unfulfilled to blessed, happy, thriving, and having more than enough!

TIMELY PROVISION

God is omniscient—He knows all things. He determined the number of the stars, and called them each by name. (See Psalm 147:4.) He knows the number of hairs on your head. (See Matthew 10:30.) David understood God's sovereignty and foreknowledge over the details of our lives, penning these words:

> *O LORD, You have searched me and known me. You know my*
> *sitting down and my rising up; You understand my thought*
> *afar off. You comprehend my path and my lying down, and*
> *are acquainted with all my ways. For there is not a word on*
> *my tongue, but behold, O LORD, You know it altogether. You*
> *have hedged me behind and before, and laid Your hand upon*
> *me. Such knowledge is too wonderful for me; it is high, I cannot*
> *attain it.*   (Psalm 139:1–6)

> *The LORD directs the steps of the godly. He delights in every*
> *detail of their lives.*   (Psalm 37:23 NLT)

> *But as for me, I trust in You, O LORD; I say, "You are my God."*
> *My times are in Your hand.*   (Psalm 31:14–15)

God has determined every man's *"preappointed times and the boundaries of their dwellings"* (Acts 17:26). He knows about us and all that concerns us, through and through. Nothing escapes His attention, including time. God is always right on time. Even when we think He's late, He's still on time because He exists outside of time. Ask Mary and Martha. They thought Jesus had messed up. He was four days late; Lazarus' body was already decomposing. Jesus went outside of time, and raised his friend from the dead. God's power can reach into time and work a miracle out of it. Time does not define God and what He does; He defines it! Even when you think that your situation is all but dead and buried and that God has missed His time, He is orchestrating and setting things up on your behalf, even when you don't see it. Come on, somebody, have faith! Don't give up! He's for you!

> EVEN WHEN YOU THINK THAT YOUR SITUATION IS ALL BUT DEAD
> AND BURIED AND THAT GOD HAS MISSED HIS TIME,
> HE IS ORCHESTRATING AND SETTING THINGS UP ON YOUR BEHALF,
> EVEN WHEN YOU DON'T SEE IT.

God's foreknowledge, wisdom, and power are too much for us to fathom, too lofty for us to grasp. I think about Moses when he complained to God about how He had the wrong guy for the job, for he was inarticulate.

> GOD got angry with Moses: *"Don't you have a brother, Aaron the Levite? He's good with words, I know he is. He speaks very well. In fact, at this very moment he's on his way to meet you."*
> (Exodus 4:14 MSG)

God never promises you anything or calls you to do anything that He hasn't already sent help and made provision for. Even before Moses started complaining, God had sent Aaron on his way to help him! I think about how God commanded the ravens to bring Elijah bread and meat *every* morning and every evening. Timely provision. Let's reflect on the faith of the centurion.

> Then Jesus said to the centurion, "Go your way; and as you have believed, so let it be done for you." And his servant was healed that same hour.   (Matthew 8:13)

He believed and recognized Jesus's authority and power to heal when and how He wanted. Right on time! Tabitha was dead, and the disciples were worried that Peter was too late. She was raised to life. The miracle took place at the time God intended.

God is fully aware of time. He is not amnesic. He hasn't forgotten the personal promises He has spoken to you. Neither has He forgotten all the promises He's made available in His Word. His integrity wouldn't allow Him to do so. God keeps His Word. He is actively watching over His Word to perform it. (See Jeremiah 1:12.)

SIX PRINCIPLES FOR TRUSTING IN GOD'S TIMING

The following story is close to my heart. I waited twenty-three years to see God's promise come to pass. My wife, Tiffany, and I married later in life, and we both had held on to the promise of marriage for many years before we met each other. We regularly meet people who are believing God for their spouse. This area of provision is significant and dear to many people's hearts. If you are single and desire to be married, this testimony will encourage you. In sharing honestly about my journey in trusting God for my marriage, my aim is to accurately represent God's faithfulness, and to highlight six general principles related to trusting in God's timing. The names mentioned in this section have been changed.

PRINCIPLE ONE: LISTEN TO GOD

I used to be Buddhist and was saved at sixteen years old. My heart was set on fire for Jesus and the gospel. I found an open room at church one Sunday morning. As I worshipped the Lord by myself in that little room, out of my mouth came the words, "Father, if it's okay with You, I'd like to serve You for the rest of my days."

What I heard next altered the course of my life.

"Son, your wife is not Asian, she's White."

"Um, what?"

I could not believe what had just happened, let alone what I had just heard. I had no grid for hearing His voice. The pagan gods and Buddha that I worshipped could not speak. I had no reason to believe that the Christian God would be any different. I thought, *This is weird. Am I hearing voices? Have I gone crazy, or was it the pizza I ate last night? This is either God or a bunch of baloney.* I kept it to myself and never told a soul.

Eight years later, a pastor came up to me and said, "I had a dream about your wedding. Your wife is not Asian, she's White."

I was so relieved. It was profound not only that God could speak, but that the Creator of the universe, the One who hung stars in space, could speak so personally and precisely into my life and my future. Listen to God concerning His promises, purposes, and provision for your life.

PRINCIPLE TWO: DON'T BE PRESUMPTUOUS

In the process of waiting, it is easy to get prideful and take matters into our hands. When the pastor told me what she saw in her dream about my wife, I could hardly contain it. I was twenty-four years old, single, and very ready to mingle. I was pumped. I bought the cologne, read the dating books, and kept my eyes wide open. Two months passed. Then two years, four years, passed. Not one White maiden remotely in sight. I was getting really frustrated.

Then came along Melanie, who was half Asian and half White. I was impatient and impulsive. I knew in my heart right from the start that it was a bad idea to date her. I did it anyway. As you can imagine, it didn't work out. When we are presumptuous and take matters into our hands instead of trusting in God's timing, we always end up with the counterfeit best. Think about Sarah, who gave her servant Hagar to Abraham as a wife because she couldn't give birth and was tired of waiting. Hagar gave birth to Ismael, who was not the chosen one with whom God would confirm his everlasting covenant. Isaac was. (See Genesis 16–17.)

PRINCIPLE THREE: DON'T GET BITTER WHILE WAITING

When God first spoke to me about my wife, I was sixteen. I did not date for twelve years till I was twenty-eight. I waited during the prime of my dating years, when I was charming and still had swag. Not one date. Really, I had dated Melanie out of presumption and out of bitterness. I told God, "I gave you the best of my youth. For twelve years, I kept myself pure, so where is my wife?" Think about the Israelites' wandering in the wilderness for forty years—what should have been an eleven-day journey. (See Deuteronomy 1:2–3.) They sinned by forgetting the Lord, complaining, rebelling, and tempting and questioning God. (See Psalm 78:12–64.) Complaints, rebellion, and bitterness not only rob our intimacy with God, but delay the fulfillment of God's promises and provision.

PRINCIPLE FOUR: DELAYS CAN BE CAUSED BY OTHERS

When things didn't work out with Melanie, I knew I had acted in rebellion. It took me awhile to realize my folly, to recover and repent from my mistake. I told myself that I was never going to repeat the same mistake again. I wanted to do it right the next time.

Then I met Suzie. She was from Germany. We were instantaneously drawn to each other, and because we both had had relationships that didn't work out, we were very careful about moving forward with our relationship. However, we both felt peace to start dating. Moreover, her parents, who were godly, discerning, and wise, gave us their approval to date. I thought I was going to marry Suzie. Things went well for six months until, one day, Suzie told me it wasn't going to work out, and decided to end the relationship.

I was mad at God. I had tried to do everything right. The Lord, in His gracious reply, said to me, *Son, even if Suzie was my will for you, she had a choice. But don't worry, I am bigger than this and I will provide a wife for you.* Sometimes, God's promises and provision are tied in to others, and delay can be caused by their action or inaction.

Nonetheless, we are to trust that God is bigger, and will work things out in spite of others.

PRINCIPLE FIVE: WE DO NOT WAIT ALONE

God is just as interested in the journey as in the destination. If our hearts stay pliable and teachable, God can refine and mature us through the waiting season. The good news is that God never asks us to wait without Him. We don't wait alone. He never leaves us to fend for ourselves. He provides the encouragement, comfort, and grace every step of the way in the waiting process. He provided companionship, fun, and support through my friends and church family during my single life. His grace is sufficient, and He provides for us in the waiting. While the children of God wandered in the wilderness for forty years, God faithfully provided for them. Their clothes and sandals didn't wear out that whole time!

> THE GOOD NEWS IS THAT GOD NEVER ASKS US TO WAIT WITHOUT HIM.... HE NEVER LEAVES US TO FEND FOR OURSELVES. HE PROVIDES THE ENCOURAGEMENT, COMFORT, AND GRACE EVERY STEP OF THE WAY IN THE WAITING PROCESS.

PRINCIPLE SIX: GOD KEEPS HIS PROMISES

From the time God spoke to me about my wife to the time I married Tiffany, my gorgeous blondie from Michigan, I waited twenty-three years. Now, that doesn't mean you will have to wait that long. Breathe easy! It was a long wait, but the promise came to pass! God kept His word. Although the waiting season has its challenges, in hindsight, I can confidently say I don't regret waiting. I am a better man because of it. I fully embraced the purposes of God in the waiting. When the promises of God come true in your life, all your frustration and pain fade into the shadows. I no longer think about the Friday nights spent watching Netflix and eating Taco Bell by myself. No! I get to behold and delight in my beautiful bride every day! When God gives you a prophetic promise, He will also give you the grace to contend for it and see it come to pass. When the waiting is long, you may be tempted to think that God has forgotten about you, your dreams, your marriage, the things He has spoken to you, or the desires He has put in your heart. Delay is not denial. Revisit the promises God has spoken to you. Keep the faith and keep believing!

God is passionate about the dreams and desires He's deposited inside of you. He's a good Father. The One who knew you before you were born, the One who created you wonderfully, is also the One who knows precisely and intimately the wonderful plans He has for you. His timing is perfect. Take your eyes off your imperfections, unbelief, doubt, and inadequacies, and set them on the One who believes in you and rejoices over you with singing. (See Zephaniah 3:17.) He loves you with relentless passion! Trust the process and have faith in the One who promised. Don't give up!

> Let us not grow weary while doing good, for in due season we
> shall reap if we do not lose heart.   (Galatians 6:9)

Here's a caveat. I don't hear God perfectly all the time. That's why I surround myself with wise counsel. Share the things that God has spoken to you with people you trust, people who know you well and have life experience with God. Sometimes, we have to admit that we have heard wrong and have the courage to move on. We can't hold God hostage to something He hasn't promised.

IN YOUR WAITING, BE CONTENT

We cannot talk about the value of waiting without also talking about contentment. Often, when God's promises don't happen according to our expectations, we get frustrated. Disappointment and discouragement, bitterness, a complaining spirit, mistrust, and even covetousness can set in like poison, contaminating and potentially snuffing out our faith. Sadly, most people don't recover from these setbacks. The antidote is contentment. Learning to live a life of faith requires us to have room in our hearts to embrace inconvenience, when things don't happen according to our terms, how we want it and when we want it. Paul learned how to live with contentment.

> *Not that I speak in regard to need, for I have learned in whatever state I am, to be content: I know how to be abased, and I know how to abound. Everywhere and in all things I have learned both to be full and to be hungry, both to abound and to suffer need. I can do all things through Christ who strengthens me.*
>
> (Philippians 4:11–13)

Paul was in prison when he wrote this and, although he was in prison, he said he was not in need. Now, Paul had been through a lot for the sake of the gospel—imprisoned, flogged, beaten, robbed, shipwrecked, you name it. He was the poster child for the persecuted Christian of his time. How he found the strength, tenacity, courage, faith, and trust to bear the weight of the afflictions and adversities is mind-boggling. Paul learned the principle of contentment; he was content in every situation and circumstance.

THE SECRET OF CONTENTMENT IS LEARNED NOT JUST IN TIMES OF SCARCITY AND LACK BUT IN TIMES OF PLENTY.

The secret of contentment is learned not just in times of scarcity and lack but in times of plenty. Perhaps you grew up in affluence and have always had everything. What would happen if everything you have ever known was suddenly taken from you? Would you be comfortable and content with little? On the other hand, maybe you come from an impoverished background, and you have always responded to lack or need in a godly manner. What, then, if wealth suddenly fell on your lap? Would the instant riches corrupt you, or would you feel guilty having incredible possessions, more than you know what to do with them?

Paul revealed that his contentment was independent of external circumstances. He had learned to anchor his heart in the goodness of God no matter what came his way, whether he was safe and secure on the shores or quivering and shivering in the storms of life. Whether he had much or little, was full or hungry, was comfortable or in despair, he approached life and, more importantly, God, the same way. He was consistent in his contentment in God, so much so that he could confidently boast, *"I can do all things through Christ who strengthens me."* This verse often has been taken out of context to refer to the ability to do anything and everything beyond a person's powers, from a kid mastering math problems without studying to running a marathon or climbing Mount Everest without training! In this context, Paul was referring to the ability to handle or cope with all situations, good or bad, prosperous or adverse circumstances, by the power of Christ.

The Greek word for *"content"* (Philippians 4:11) in Paul's passage here is used by the Stoics to mean self-sufficiency and independence from others. Strength and virtue are found within oneself.[1] That's why we would use the word *stoic* to describe someone who can endure pain or hardship without showing feelings or complaining. Quite the contrary, Paul used the same word to denote strength and virtue without himself, indicating his utter confidence and reliance on Christ. Paul was not so much self-sufficient as God-sufficient.

> *Not that we are sufficient of ourselves to think of anything as being from ourselves, but our sufficiency is from God.*
>
> (2 Corinthians 3:5)

Another area of contentment that is often tested is finances. Trusting God for our provision is often related to finances. Paul teaches that we are not to be enticed by money but to learn to be content with what we have.

> *Let your character [your moral essence, your inner nature] be free from the love of money [shun greed—be financially ethical], being content with what you have; for He has said, "I WILL NEVER [under any circumstances] DESERT YOU [nor give you up nor leave you without support, nor will I in any degree leave you helpless], NOR WILL I FORSAKE or LET YOU DOWN or RELAX*

My hold on you [assuredly not]!" So we take comfort and are encouraged and confidently say, "The Lord is my Helper [in time of need], I will not be afraid. What will man do to me?" (Hebrews 13:5–6 amp)

Discontentment often leads to covetousness. We become disgruntled, envious, and jealous of what others have. We take our eyes off the sufficiency of Christ. If we are not careful, it can poison our hearts, erode our trust in God, and, ultimately, snuff out the blessings of God in our lives. We deal with covetousness and fear or lack by establishing a contentment that is built on God's promise to provide for our daily needs. It fills us with confidence so we can declare, "God is able to make all grace abound to me, so that, having sufficiency in all things at all times, I will abound in every good work." (See 2 Corinthians 9:8.)

PRAYER OF FAITH

Father, thank You that my times and seasons are in Your hands. You made everything beautiful in Your perfect timing. You're the God of the details, and nothing escapes your attention. You are the Alpha and Omega, the First and the Last. You have full knowledge of what, when, where, and how things should happen. Your foreknowledge and wisdom are beyond my comprehension. With faith and patience, I will inherit all the promises, breakthroughs, and provision You have prepared for my life. I fully embrace and trust Your timing. Amen!

10

THE POWER OF STEWARDSHIP

"Every faculty you have, your power of thinking or of
moving your limbs from moment to moment, is given you
by God. If you devoted every moment of your whole life
exclusively to His service, you could not give Him anything
that was not in a sense His own already."
—C. S. Lewis, *Mere Christianity*

Kingdom provision requires that we steward well what God gives to
us. It's in stewarding well that God enlarges our capacity to receive
more from Him. In His sovereign wisdom, He provides for the needs
of His children and the kingdom. Many believers underestimate the
importance God places on stewardship. The Bible begins and ends
with the theme of stewardship. In Genesis, God commanded Adam
and Eve to *"be fruitful and multiply; fill the earth and subdue it; have
dominion over the fish of the sea, over the birds of the air, and over every
living thing that moves on the earth"* (Genesis 1:28). God also put
Adam in the garden of Eden *"to tend and keep it"* (Genesis 2:15). In
Revelation, Jesus promised, *"My reward is with Me, to give to every one
according to his work"* (Revelation 22:12).

God, who *"created the heavens and the earth"* (Genesis 1:1), has
the absolute right of ownership over all things in His kingdom. *"The
earth is the LORD's, and all its fullness, the world and those who dwell*

therein" (Psalm 24:1). We have been called to be stewards and care-takers, tasked with managing His resources till He comes again. Kingdom stewardship requires our practical obedience in administrating everything God has entrusted into our care—time, energy, health, money, material possessions, resources, jobs, talents, spiritual gifts, dreams and aspirations, relationships, and family. It is an act of consecrating our lives and what He's given to us for His kingdom purpose and service. It demands that we relinquish the right of control of our resources to God. He is the owner and source of all things. When we accede to this kingdom principle, we can accurately view and responsibly manage our lives and resources.

God provides good gifts for His children. (See James 1:17.) He has given us all that we need to fulfill our role and potential here on earth. Second Peter 1:3 says, "*His divine power has given to us all things that pertain to life and godliness.*" That is His gift to us. The manner and attitude with which we steward that is our gift back to Him.

> A LOT OF OUR MONEY CHALLENGES AND STRESS COULD BE AVOIDED IF WE LEAN ON GOD FOR HIS WISDOM, PRACTICED SELF-CONTROL, AND GOOD STEWARDSHIP.

In my conversations with people about God's provision, they often tell me something like this: "Cornelius, you say that God provides for all of our needs. I trusted God for rent this month, and He didn't show up." They get upset at God. Often, I find out after chatting with them that the reason they couldn't pay their rent or bills is because they have been reckless with their spending. Suppose a person has seven hundred dollars before the next payday, his rent is due in a few days, and he impulsively spends five hundred dollars on a weekend shopping spree, leaving him short of rent money. Well, that's not God's fault. That's poor arithmetic and bad stewardship. God regularly gets the blame for a lot of things He has nothing to do with. Often, we don't seek God on how we should be spending our money, and it comes back to bite us. I believe that a lot of our money challenges and stress could be avoided if we lean on God for His wisdom, practiced self-control, and good stewardship.

All provision, including our finances, come from God. But we are responsible for their use. I am grateful that God, in His grace and mercy, often covers up our messes. He still comes through despite our mistakes, but we can't hold God to ransom and expect Him to bail us out every time when we fail to seek His counsel in how we spend our money.

A WORD ABOUT DEBT

Because of bad stewardship, many have gotten into trouble with mountains of debt. America is characterized by excessive spending and is riddled with debt. Mortgages, car loans, credit card payments, college loans, house insurance, car insurance, health insurance, phone bills, utility bills, doctor bills, and so forth. Credit card debt alone is staggering. According to a report by Bloomberg, America's household credit card debt was $747 billion in the third quarter of 2016, and was projected to reach $842 billion by 2019, based on data from the Federal Reserve Bank of New York.[1]

Our generation is accustomed to living with debt. It is a normal part of life in America, and we are drowning under the weight and stress of it. Many families are on the brink of bankruptcy. Most people end up paying a lot of money in interest just to service the debt. With large amounts of money going to bankers, mortgage lenders, and credit card companies, Christians in debt find that their ability to provide for themselves and their families, and their freedom to pursue kingdom purposes, has been significantly diminished.

God does not want His people to be in debt. In the Old Testament, we see how debt can have serious consequences. Because of debt, the children of Israel lost much of their land and possessions. Moreover, some of them had to sell themselves or their children into slavery to pay their debts. (See Nehemiah 5:3–5.) This was reflected in the story of the widow who came to Elisha and said, *"Your servant my husband is dead, and you know that your servant feared the LORD.*

And the creditor is coming to take my two sons to be his slaves" (2 Kings 4:1). In the New Testament, Paul tells us that we are to "owe no one anything except to love one another" (Romans 13:8).

Incurring debt is not categorically wrong. Credit cards can be useful and convenient while, at the same time, misused and abused. Unless you can manage them wisely and have a plan and the ability to make payments and pay off credit debt entirely, you should consider cutting them up. Don't spend what you don't have and don't buy stuff you can't afford. The same principle applies to buying a house or a car. When debt becomes a detriment to our spiritual life and kingdom priorities, God does not permit. Here's how debt can negatively affect us:

1. Debt can cause so much stress, worry, anxiety, and fear that it affects our relationship with the Lord.

2. Debt can limit our ability and freedom to give and bless others.

3. Debt can stop us from pursuing the dreams God has given to us. I have met many believers who, because of debt, are not able to fulfill the dream of starting a business or going to the mission field.

4. Debt can strain family relationships. Financial stress is a primary reason for family arguments and divorce. Also, many families cannot go on vacations and spend quality time and fun together because of financial constraints.

5. Debt can keep parents from leaving an inheritance for their children. (See Proverbs 13:22.)

Follow God's wisdom and honor Him in your spending. Determine that you are going to be a good steward of God's resources. When we are faithful with what we have, God will enlarge our capacity to have more.

STEWARDING NEEDS VERSUS DESIRES

There are generally three groups of people when it comes to believing in God as Provider. The first group are those who do not believe that God will provide for all their needs. The second group believes that God can and will provide for all their needs. The third group believes that God not only wants to provide for their needs but for their desires as well.

WHAT WE BELIEVE ABOUT GOD PROVIDING FOR OUR NEEDS OR DESIRES WILL AFFECT HOW WE RECEIVE AND STEWARD HIS PROVISION.

What we believe about God providing for our needs or desires will affect how we receive and steward His provision. Let's get a basic Christian understanding about need and desire. A need is a basic, essential thing we must have to live and accomplish God's will for our lives. A desire is that which brings us great satisfaction, delight, and pleasure. I have met many people who believe that God wants to meet only their essential needs. Their premise is that if they ask God for something that they desire but don't need, God will not be interested in granting it. This belief is not congruous with the tenor of the gospel message.

John 10:10 says, *"The thief does not come except to steal, and to kill, and to destroy. I have come that they may have life, and that they may have it more abundantly."* God is not a killjoy who's always ready to put a dampener on anything that is fun and enjoyable to us. He wants us to enjoy the abundant life that He provides. What father would want his children to barely make it and not be able to enjoy the finer things in life? As humans, we may have limited resources, but God and His resources have no limits. He is a God of abundance. God desires that we not only survive and have the bare minimum in life but thrive, have more than enough so that our basic needs are met, get to enjoy the nice things in life, and have surplus to bless others.

Some religious people think we should be holy, somber, and disassociated from anything fun, desirous, and pleasurable. They perceive these as worldly pursuits. Worldly people just let their desires run wild. They can care less about holy living. Liberated people in God live holy lives and enjoy them at the same time! Living in holiness and the freedom to enjoy life don't have to be polarized from each other. Ask God for the desires of your heart, as well as what you need!

> *Delight yourself also in the* LORD, *and He shall give you the desires of your heart.*   (Psalm 37:4)

Herein is the caveat: The condition upon which God gives us the desires of our hearts is that we delight in Him. God does not honor the desires of our hearts that do not honor Him. He does not grant us the desires that keep us from fulfilling His plan, dream, and purpose for our lives. Neither will He give us the desires that will cause us harm.

> *You say, "I am allowed to do anything"—but not everything is good for you. You say, "I am allowed to do anything"—but not everything is beneficial.*   (1 Corinthians 10:23 NLT)

GOD'S IDEA FOR WORK

One of the ways in which we steward God's provision for our lives is through our capacity and ability to work. God established the value and role of work at the beginning. God tasked Adam and Eve with the ongoing management and cultivation of His creation. Work is not only one of the means through which God provides our basic needs and things to enjoy, it is itself a gift from Him. It is part of our identity and responsibility while we are here on earth. Proverbs 13:11 says, *"Wealth gained by dishonesty will be diminished, but he who gathers by labor will increase."* Paul also has some strong words about working and providing for the family. *"If anyone does not provide for his own, and especially for those of his household, he has denied the faith and is worse than an unbeliever"* (1 Timothy 5:8). Moreover, Paul exhorts all of Jesus's followers to work, to do *"something useful with their own hands, that they may have something to share with those in need"* (Ephesians 4:28 NIV). Kingdom perspective and motivation for work includes helping and sharing with others what we have.

No doubt God can provide supernaturally. The Bible is full of miraculous stories of provision. When the children of Israel were in the wilderness for forty years, neither their clothes nor sandals wore out. (See Deuteronomy 29:5.) God sent the ravens to feed Elijah. (See 1 Kings 17:4.) There was an abundant supply of oil for the prophet's widow. (See 2 Kings 4:1–7.) God multiplied the fish and bread to feed the multitudes. (See Matthew 14:13–21.) Jesus and Peter's temple tax was paid by a gold coin found in a fish's mouth (see Matthew 17:27). And so forth.

God also provides naturally, through the work of our hands. I have met believers and those in the ministry who believe that if they could muster enough faith in God's ability to meet their needs, they wouldn't have to work to provide sustenance. Work is not a second-class, less spiritual option in our journey of trusting God for provision. Paul himself worked as a tentmaker, an example to those who might think that a person in ministry has a right to be lazy or mooch off other people. From God's perspective, we need to be the best stewards of our gifts and talents, wherever He's placed us and whatever He's called us to accomplish in the kingdom. I believe that we should pray that God provides us with a job that's most compatible with the talents, gifting, and calling He's placed in our lives. That's where the dreams and purposes God has for our lives will flourish, where we will be most effective and influential for the kingdom. We are bearers of His glory and integrity no matter where we are. We need to take pride in our work and carry a spirit of excellence so that the Lord can shine through us and be glorified at our workplaces.

Hard work and diligence at our jobs, recognizing that God is the source of all provision, can lead to great favor, abundance, prosperity, and provision. Consider these Scriptures:

May the favor of the Lord our God rest on us; establish the work of our hands for us—yes, establish the work of our hands.
(Psalm 90:17 NIV)

Those who work their land will have abundant food, but those who chase fantasies have no sense. (Proverbs 12:11 NIV)

Lazy people want much but get little, but those who work hard will prosper. (Proverbs 13:4 NLT)

Work brings profit, but mere talk leads to poverty! (Proverbs 14:23 NLT)

Whatever you do, work at it with all your heart, as working for the Lord, not for human masters, since you know that you will receive an inheritance from the Lord as a reward. It is the Lord Christ you are serving. (Colossians 3:23–24 NIV)

Go to the ant, you sluggard! Consider her ways and be wise, which, having no captain, overseer or ruler, provides her supplies in the summer, and gathers her food in the harvest. How long will you slumber, O sluggard? When will you rise from your sleep? A little sleep, a little slumber, a little folding of the hands to sleep—so shall your poverty come on you like a prowler, and your need like an armed man. (Proverbs 6:6–11)

STEWARDING YOUR GOD-GIVEN DREAMS AND CALLING

Some of us dream and aspire to be doctors, scientists, police officers, firefighters, actors or actresses, dancers, or to own a successful business, start a restaurant, run a nonprofit to eradicate human trafficking, and so forth. God wants us to steward those dreams and aspirations that are connected to His kingdom purpose. Every believer is called to be a Christ ambassador to bring His presence, love, and power to every sphere of society, not just within the church.

When was I newly saved, I thought that if a person wanted to be godly, spiritual, and a bona fide Christian, he had to pursue the call to be a pastor or a missionary. That's what he had to do. God was interested only in getting souls into heaven. He didn't have the time for our dreams to start a business, run a restaurant, or be a marine biologist. The way I thought affected the way I viewed God's provision. I believed that God was inclined to provide only ministry-related things or that which yielded spiritual results. It took several years for me to be set free from that religious mind-set.

The truth is that God wants to provide for the actress who's stewarding her God-given dream and calling to influence Hollywood just as much as the missionary He's called to influence the nations. When we discover the kingdom purpose and calling behind our God-given dreams and aspirations, we can boldly and confidently believe God's provision for them will be fulfilled. My good friend Jon did just that. Here's his amazing testimony:

> God put a dream in my heart to create an application to simplify a complex task. Jesus is all about simplicity, which is why He asked us to become like little children to enter His kingdom. Since launching the application business, I have seen miraculous provision in key areas. However, raising or growing the finances to develop the product further had always been a huge challenge. In 2015, several years after the launch, our cash flow became a crisis. By November, it was money in, money out, every day. We were just barely staying afloat. With a very heavy heart, I finally laid off two members of staff for the business to survive.
>
> Early in December, one of my dearest friends—halfway around the world—woke up one night with the figure of £15,000 in her head. She prayed specifically that certain members of my family would invest that sum into my business. That morning, my friend and her husband agreed in prayer for this to happen.
>
> What my friend did not know was that I'd had ongoing conversations with relatives for many months about investing in my business. However, no figure had ever been discussed and, to be honest, because things had moved so slowly, I had almost given up hope that it would happen.
>
> However, about ten days after my friends prayed, my relatives informed me that they were investing exactly £15,000 into my business. They had decided and were happy to do it

immediately. A few days later, the funds were transferred to my account, and that investment put my business on a solid footing again! I was totally amazed by the grace of God, His perfect timing, and the sheer simplicity of answered prayer. It was such a clear and specific sign from my heavenly Papa: He was backing the business and the dream He had given me!

A REWARD MENTALITY

Paul tells us that we all will appear before Christ one day, and He will judge everything we have done, good or bad. (See 2 Corinthians 5:10.) Like the servants in the parable of the talents (see Matthew 25:14–30), we will be called to give an account for how we have managed what the Master has given to us.

In that parable, the first two servants were diligent and faithful, investing and multiplying what had been entrusted to them. They were duly rewarded with more. In contrast, the third servant was inactive and lazy. The Master came and took away what had been given to him. The servant's excuse was this:

> Lord, I knew you to be a hard man, reaping where you have not sown, and gathering where you have not scattered seed. And I was afraid, and went and hid your talent in the ground. Look, there you have what is yours.   (Matthew 25:24–25)

As a young Christian, I remember listening to sermons about this lazy servant and thinking to myself, *I can totally relate to the dude. The Master is a shrewd taskmaster. I wouldn't have worked for Him, either!* But that's exactly how I perceived the Lord—the celestial slave driver who would have me rise before the crack of dawn, work all day and night, head back to the slave's quarters, get three hours of shut-eye on a wooden plank bed, and start it over the next day. You get the picture. No, thank you! It was no wonder I had no joy, desire, or motivation to serve the Lord. The reality is that many people view God that way.

Some years later, the Lord began to change my perspective. He said to me, "Son, I don't want you just to be responsible; I want you to be rewarded. It's not just about you working for Me; I am also working on your behalf. When you steward what I have given to you well, I will give you more. I am not taking from you; I'm giving to you."

The Lord began to speak to me about having a "reward" mentality. He said, "Son, there is a reward attached to every yes and every act of obedience and diligence you do to Me."

> MANY OF US NEED TO SHIFT FROM A "RESPONSIBLE SLAVE" TO A "REWARDED STEWARD" MENTALITY. EVEN EARTHLY PARENTS KNOW HOW TO REWARD THEIR CHILDREN. HOW MUCH MORE DOES THE HEAVENLY FATHER KNOW HOW TO REWARD US!

It revolutionized the way I viewed and served Him. Now, when the Lord calls and gives me an assignment, I no longer grudgingly say yes out of obligation. I do it out of delight and anticipation that I will be rewarded with joy and so much more! And guess what? I began to see an increase in the level of favor, blessings, opportunities, and provision in my life. Many of us need to shift from a "responsible slave" to a "rewarded steward" mentality. Even earthly parents know how to reward their children. How much more does the heavenly Father know how to reward us! You will be duly rewarded for your diligent stewardship and faithful obedience!

Well done, good and faithful servant; you were faithful over a few things, I will make you ruler over many things. Enter into the joy of your lord.   (Matthew 25:21)

MY PRAYER AGREEMENT WITH YOU

Not too long ago, the Spirit gave me a prophetic word and assignment for the body of Christ. He said to me: "I want you to pray and come into agreement with the saints of God concerning the seeds that they have sown (including time, ministry, finances, resources, every act of sacrifice, love, compassion, and so forth). The body of Christ needs to know that there are rewards attached to every seed of faith and obedience they have sown. Believers need to move from a slave mind-set to a reward mind-set. Many have sacrificed and have said yes in obedience concerning the things the Lord has spoken to them, yet many are slow and passive in anticipating and believing for the harvest. Tell them to release the spirit of celebration and joy over every act, every seed that they have sown for the kingdom, and watch what I'll do. I will multiply time, rest, and resources back to them! I am their shield and their exceedingly great reward!"

The Lord gave me a picture and showed me that whenever a believer says yes to the Lord in obedience, heaven is moved, and an immediate supernatural momentum is released in the Spirit. Angels are assigned and dispatched to bring about the harvest of the seeds of obedience. A slave mind-set is slow to anticipate the goodness and kindness of God. When I sow a seed, I am quick to celebrate and release joy and faith over it, believing that something is set into motion and that the rewards of heaven are on their way!

PRAYER OF FAITH

It is only fitting that I take the opportunity to pray and come into agreement with you.

Father, thank you that You have called us to be stewards of your kingdom resources. I come into agreement now with my brothers and sisters who have sown seeds of diligence, faith, and faithful obedience to the things You have called them to. I pray that heaven will be open over them and that the joy, blessings, and rewards of heaven will be released over their lives. We thank You, Lord, and celebrate You for being a generous Father, Provider, and Rewarder to us! Amen!

11

STEWARDING THE REVELATION

"Jesus taught men to see the operation of God in the regular and the normal—in the rising of the sun and the falling of the rain and the growth of the plant."
—William Temple

Just as important as stewarding God's resources is stewarding the revelation of God's nature and character. The psalmist says, *"Blessed and favored by God are those who keep His testimonies, and who [consistently] seek Him and long for Him with all their heart"* (Psalm 119:2 AMP). *"His testimonies"* refer to His ways, His Word, and His precepts, that is, the divine revelation of who God is. Paul instructs us that, *"as servants of Christ and stewards of the mysteries of God.... It is required in stewards that one be found faithful"* (1 Corinthians 4:1–2). When we are faithful to keep and steward the divine revelation of God and seek Him with diligent hearts, we position ourselves to receive His blessings and favor.

> *Anyone who wants to come to him must believe that God exists and that he rewards those who sincerely seek him.*
>
> (Hebrews 11:6 NLT)

Biblical economics and prosperity are not measured by what's in your wallet, how much you have in your bank account, how many assets you own, or by what you have or don't have. It is measured by how well you steward the revelation that God is your Source and Provider. It is stewarding what He's given to us and, more significantly, who He's given and revealed to us. The almighty God, the one who has created and sustains the universe, the Chief Shepherd who owns *"the cattle on a thousand hills"* (Psalm 50:10), has chosen to give all of Himself to us. Mind blown! Who but God can aptly and fittingly introduce Himself as *"I AM WHO I AM"* (Exodus 3:14)? He is everything that He says He is! He will be who He says He will be! And we experience the totality of who God is, His fullness, in our lives, now and for eternity. We grow and increase in our experiential knowledge of Him until we see Him face-to-face on that day!

The way to grow our faith is to steward the revelation and character of God well. They are directly related. We experience God and His providential care to the degree we steward His nature and revelation. God is the source of all provision over our lives. Declare with me: "The Lord is my source!" Now say that 327 times, or until it resonates in your spirit! He is a covenant-keeping God. Covenant with God is a mutual blessing. God receives us, His people, as His inheritance, and we receive God, our Father, as our inheritance. We get to receive all that God is—His essence, His attributes, His nature, His providential care, and so much more!

JEHOVAH JIREH

Perhaps no other name of God is more pertinent to this book than *Jehovah Jireh.*

> *Abraham called the name of that place Jehovahjireh: as it is said to this day, in the mount of the LORD it shall be seen.*
> (Genesis 22:14 KJV)

In Hebrew, Jehovah Jireh is translated "the Lord will provide" or "the Lord sees."[1] The name was mentioned in the context of God asking Abraham to sacrifice his son Isaac. When Isaac asked his dad where the sheep was for the burnt offering, Abraham replied, *"Son, God will see to it that there's a sheep for the burnt offering"* (Genesis 22:8 MSG).

Stewarding the Revelation 167

Abraham didn't know how God was going to show up. He simply believed that He would. He had faith in God's infinite wisdom, knowledge, and power to provide.

> HOW YOU PERCEIVE GOD DETERMINES HOW YOU RECEIVE FROM HIM. HE IS JEHOVAH JIREH, NOT JEHOVAH MISER! HE SEES OUR NEEDS, AND HE WILL PROVIDE!

If you believe the Lord is Jehovah Jireh, then believe in His infinite capacity and power to supply all your needs, His infinite wisdom to know when and how to provide, and His infinite knowledge of all your needs before you even utter them. How you perceive Him determines how you receive from Him. He is Jehovah Jireh, not Jehovah Miser! He sees our needs, and He will provide!

BELIEVING OVER AND OVER AGAIN

Abram, who became Abraham, understood and stewarded well the revelation that God was His source and the covenant-keeping God. In Genesis 14, the king of Sodom and his allies were defeated by the invaders from the east, and he had lost all his goods, provisions, and people. Abram's nephew Lot and his goods were taken as well. When Abram heard that his nephew had been taken captive, he and his armed servants fought the invaders, and recovered all the goods, his nephew Lot and his goods, as well as the womenfolk and the people. (See Genesis 14:1–16.)

The first thing that Abram did was tithe to Melchizedek, king of Salem and priest of El-Elyon, or God Most High. (See Genesis 14:20.) He is an antetype of Jesus Christ in His role as King and Priest. Melchizedek means "my king is righteous or legitimate."[2] Melchizedek blesses Abram, and Abram, in turn, responds and submits to the king and priest Melchizedek by paying him a tithe, thereby recognizing his status. Abram tithed because he recognized he didn't own the spoils; he was just stewarding them temporarily.

In the same way, we tithe to our Lord, our King and Priest Jesus, the righteous and legitimate One, because we recognize that all blessings come from Him. He alone is our source, and all we have is His.

Second, the king of Sodom told Abram to keep the goods for himself but to return the people. (See Genesis 14:21.) Notice Abram's outstanding reply:

> I have raised my hand to the LORD, God Most High, the Possessor of heaven and earth, that I will take nothing, from a thread to a sandal strap, and that I will not take anything that is yours, lest you should say, "I have made Abram rich"—except only what the young men have eaten, and the portion of the men who went with me: Aner, Eshcol, and Mamre; let them take their portion." (Genesis 14:22–24)

After giving a tenth of the spoils to Melchizedek, Abram gave the remaining to the king of Sodom. If we were there at the scene, this is the declaration I imagine we would hear from Abram:

> My worship and my allegiance belong to Yahweh, El-Elyon, my God the Most High, the One to whom I owe my life and my existence. He is the Possessor of heaven and earth. He alone is the fount of every blessing and provision. I solemnly swear to my God that I will not take any of the spoils, lest it is said that I profited in my own strength. Yahweh alone is my source!

Third, Abram made sure that his allies, Aner, Eschol, and Mamre, got to keep their share of the spoils. (See Genesis 14:24.) He did not impose his decision to forgo his share of the spoils on them. A person who lives with the acknowledgment and revelation that God alone is the source of all blessings and provision never hoards everything for himself. He is generous as the Father is generous.

It is remarkable that Genesis 15, God's monumental covenant-cutting ceremony with Abram, follows immediately after this. This is where God established Himself as the Covenant-Keeper, who made an oath before heaven and earth to provide for Abram and His people forever. I believe that because Abram stood the test and faithfully stewarded the revelation that God was His source, God rewarded him with an extraordinary promise: *"I am your shield, your exceedingly great reward"* (Genesis 15:1).

God took him outside, and as they looked up at the array of incalculable stars, the One who flung each one of them into space made another startling promise to Abram: *"So shall your descendants be"* (Genesis 15:5).

Abram *"believed in the LORD, and He accounted it to him for righteousness"* (Genesis 15:6). The Hebrew verb translated *"believed"* here indicates repeated or continuing action, meaning "he kept on believing."[3] Abram continued stewarding and believing the revelation that God was his source, covenant provider, and a keeper of His word, over and over again. He never stopped recognizing who God was— His goodness, His kindness, and His faithfulness. Abram's faith was enduring, constant, and unwavering. When doubts came, he believed. When worries and anxieties came, he raised his hands, worshiped, and still believed. When opportunities came to second-guess God's goodness and promises, he stood his ground and kept on believing!

> ON THE JOURNEY OF FAITH, IT IS NOT SO MUCH ABOUT PRAYING MORE, FASTING MORE, OR DOING MORE; IT'S ABOUT STANDING STRONG. DIG YOUR HEELS IN DEEP AND STAND FIRM ON THE REVELATION OF GOD'S NATURE AND CHARACTER.

On the journey of faith, it is not so much about praying more, fasting more, or doing more; it's about standing strong. Dig your heels in deep and stand firm on the revelation of God's nature and character. That's how you stand and combat the enemy when he throws a barrage of lies at you to corrupt God's truth of who He is. (See Ephesians 6:13.)

THE POWER OF REMEMBRANCE

To steward a revelation is to reflect and meditate on it, to chew the cud, and to remember it over and over until the truth of who God is resonates within your spirit. Remembering was a key principle in the Old Testament. God consistently protected, provided, and delivered the Israelites in times of crisis. Over and again, when the times were good, the Israelites forgot that the Lord had come through and performed miracles on their behalf. (See Deuteronomy 6:10–12; 8:10–14; Judges 8:33–34.)

God promised the Israelites to provide for them by giving them the capacity and ability to acquire resources to meet their needs.

> *Remember the LORD your God, for it is He who gives you power to get wealth, that He may establish His covenant which He swore to your fathers, as it is this day.*   (Deuteronomy 8:18)

God's revelation to the Israelites as the source and provider of all things confirmed the covenant that He was making with them. He reaffirmed His providential care for them. God's promise to His people was not scarcity but sufficiency. However, the Lord prefaced His promise with a condition to remember. The weight of this is reflected in God's warning to them: If they were to "*forget the LORD* [their] *God, and follow other gods, and serve them and worship them… [they] shall surely perish*" (Deuteronomy 8:19).

Every blessing we enjoy is a direct result of God as the covenant-keeper, and the outcome of His promise to our forefathers. Wealth and prosperity cannot be considered a natural right. It is a gift from God, not an entitlement. When we slip into entitlement mode, we start to forget that the blessings of God are His gracious gifts to us.

Perhaps God's command to remember the Lord was most tested when the Israelites were in the wilderness and the Promised Land. Their hearts were peeled back and revealed. In the wilderness, they were challenged in their faith and trust during a time of lack. The revelation of God as their Shepherd and sole Provider was put to the test. Think about the difficulties the Israelites had to endure: heat, sand, snakes, scorpions, hunger, thirst. In such conditions, they were probably tempted to ask, "If God really loves us, why is all this happening?" They were having pity parties. On the other hand, when they were delivered into the Promised Land, they were tested again in a time of abundance. Similarly, the revelation of God as the origin and source of their provision was tested. They may have been tempted to say, *"My power and the might of my hand have gained me this wealth"* (Deuteronomy 8:17). Pride and self-pity are just as detrimental to our relationship with the Lord.

When the Israelites crossed the Jordan River to enter the Promised Land, Joshua called each of the tribes to gather a large stone from the river and, using these twelve stones, they built a memorial to the faithfulness of God. He understood the power of remembrance. These memorial stones not only serve to remind the Israelites what God had done on their behalf, but they also served as a reminder to the next generation of the mighty power of God. God had done some amazing things that Joshua knew should not ever be forgotten. He supplied their every need in the desert for forty years. He provided manna every morning, quail in the evenings, and water from a rock, and their clothes and sandals never wore out!

Forgetting, or not remembering, the Lord is not simply a matter of amnesia. When we do so, we risk losing the history of our relationship with Him, all that He's done for us in the good and the challenging times. We all have experienced pain and hurt when we lose touch with or feel forgotten by a special friend or family member with whom we have shared significant history. It is no different with the Lord. He feels the pain, rejection, and betrayal when we forget His constant care and provision for our lives. The Israelites were tempted to be prideful and ignore that God had saved them (Deuteronomy 8:14), led them (verse 15), watered them (verse 15), fed them (verse 16), and gifted them (verse 18).

In 2009, after turning down a ministry position at an influential church in Palo Alto, California, I went on an extended fast, seeking the Lord for direction concerning my next season in ministry.

The Lord said, "Son, I want you to pioneer a ministry from scratch, and I'm giving you the vision for it."

I wish I could tell you I was over the moon about the proposition. It was not music to my ears. I actually dreaded it. I dreaded the thought that I would have to build everything from ground zero, and how much blood, sweat, and tears would be shed in the process. I cringed at the thought that I wasn't ready for the hard work and the faith that were needed to do it well. My excuse was that I didn't have any money or resources to do it.

I told Him, "No, Lord. Find someone else to do it."

I wasn't ready for what happened next.

"Son, when have I ever failed you or not provided for you?"

"Lord, I am sure I can think of one time when You've either not shown up or shown up really late!"

> OUR REMEMBRANCE OF WHAT GOD HAS DONE IN THE PAST SHAPES OUR PERSPECTIVE IN THE PRESENT.
> WE ARE ESSENTIALLY PROPHESYING AND RELEASING THE TESTIMONY OF HIS NATURE, HIS POWER, AND HIS PROVISION FOR OUR PRESENT LIVES, NEEDS, AND CIRCUMSTANCES.

I replied with such cockiness, heaven must had been repulsed. Alas, the mighty man of faith and power was reduced to the man of paste and flour. As soon as I said it, the Holy Spirit began to remind me of acts of the Father's benevolence, breakthrough, and provision in my life, one after another. Testimonies of His goodness swirled in my head, and were brought to the forefront of my mind. This went on for nearly two hours. Tears streamed down my cheeks as I remembered and revisited God's faithful provision in my life over the last fifteen years. He was never late, and He never failed to show up. Not once.

Prostrate and humbled before the Lord, I declared, "Lord, You've been faithful. You've done it all these years. You can do it all over again!"

Subsequently, the ministry of 7K was birthed.

Remembering the Lord is not just a mental or perfunctory exercise. It's a relinquishing of our self-sufficiency and a recommitting of ourselves to Him all over again. We acknowledge who He is, and remind ourselves of what He has done and can do on our behalf. Our remembrance of what God has done in the past shapes our perspective in the present. We are essentially prophesying and releasing the testimony of His nature, His power, and His provision for our present lives, needs, and circumstances. We pull from God's proven track record and release it into the now!

Most Christians undermine the weight God places on this matter. Forgetting God is tantamount to disobedience, understood as a failure to observe God's commands.

> Beware that you do not forget the LORD your God by not keeping His commandments, His judgments, and His statutes which I command you today, lest—when you have eaten and are full, and have built beautiful houses and dwell in them; and when your herds and your flocks multiply, and your silver and your gold are multiplied, and all that you have is multiplied; when your heart is lifted up, and you forget the LORD your God who brought you out of the land of Egypt, from the house of bondage.
>
> (Deuteronomy 8:11–14)

From God's perspective, we can enjoy material and financial blessings while still being disobedient. On the flip side, remembering God is considered an act of obedience, and we are always rewarded when we obey.

So, to remember the Lord, to steward the revelation that He is the source of all provision, is the chief principle of biblical economics. We must constantly be reminded that God's promised to give us the power and ability to get wealth—to provide for us and His kingdom purposes (not for greed and self-indulgence)—when He established His covenant with us. (See Deuteronomy 8:18.) At the same time, God warned us that there will be dire consequences if we forget or forsake Him and pursue other idols. The Father's love is jealous for us. He is secure and confident in His providential care for His children. No one can provide as well as He can. For our own good as well as for His glory, He will not allow His place to be taken by another. There is only one divine Provider and Father of all good gifts!

STEWARDING A PROSPEROUS MIND-SET

Contrary to what some might think, prosperity is more than wealth and riches. It relates to all areas of our lives. God's definition of prosperity involves the whole person—spiritually, mentally, emotionally, physically, financially, and relationally. The word *salvation* means more than a ticket to heaven. It is translated from the Greek word *soteria*, and it means to save, deliver, protect, heal, preserve, do well, and to make whole.[4]

We all know of people who have wealth and riches and yet are struggling in some areas of their lives. We regularly read about highly influential and wealthy leaders, politicians, CEOs, and celebrities who are in the news for all the wrong reasons. God desires that each of us prospers and is whole, and lives a healthy, balanced, and fruitful life.

The Bible seems to connect our inner world and our outer world. The wise King Solomon put it this way: *"Keep your heart with all diligence, for out of it spring the issues of life"* (Proverbs 4:23). Third John 1:2 says, *"Beloved, I pray that you may prosper in all things and be in health, just as your soul prospers."* We can't fully prosper materially and physically unless we are also prospering spiritually. Jesus says, *"For what profit is it to a man if he gains the whole world, and loses his own soul? Or what will a man give in exchange for his soul?"* (Matthew 16:26). One of the signs of the end times is a preoccupation with riches and wealth. (See Revelation 18:9–19.) Many will sacrifice their faith at the altar of the unrelenting pursuit of wealth. If a person ends up having all the power and wealth in the earth and rejects Jesus, he remains a poor person. Jesus was prioritizing what really matters eternally, one's soul and right relationship with Christ. Everything the world has to offer will eventually fade away—fame, riches, prestige, power, and so forth. When we prioritize correctly and obey the Lord, He can and will bless us. (See Matthew 6:33.) Blessings, provision, and prosperity will follow according to the way God designed and intended. It is part of the covenant God made with His people. (See Deuteronomy 28:1–14.)

> So you shall serve the LORD your God, and He will bless your bread and your water. And I will take sickness away from the midst of you.   (Exodus 23:25)

> In that I command you today to love the LORD your God, to walk in His ways, and to keep His commandments, His statutes, and His judgments, that you may live and multiply; and the LORD your God will bless you in the land which you go to possess.   (Deuteronomy 30:16)

Wealth and riches are neutral; they are not evil in and of themselves. God is not against His people gaining wealth, but He is displeased when His people gain riches at the expense of other areas of their lives. A life with out-of-order priorities is destined for frustration and failure, not success and prosperity.

A WORD ABOUT PROSPERITY

Few words make believers cringe like *money*, *riches*, and *prosperity*. Often, the mention of these words evokes strong emotions, contempt, and criticism. Ministers who talk about money or prosperity are shot down immediately by some irate Christians. They think that the messages that these ministers preach target their wallets, not their hearts. These ministers are quickly squashed in a box and slapped shut with the label "prosperity preachers" or "money mongers." Regrettably, a lot of this is attributed to the abuse many have observed, seen, taught, or experienced. One thing is for sure: A gospel that is focused on getting rich and serving self is not the gospel Jesus taught or came to show us.

> ## A GOSPEL THAT IS FOCUSED ON GETTING RICH AND SERVING SELF IS NOT THE GOSPEL JESUS TAUGHT OR CAME TO SHOW US.

I have observed something interesting about prosperity slayers. Some Christians are quick to criticize the prosperity preachers camp but wouldn't have a problem praying for bills to be paid, food on the table, a better job, a new car or house, or a nice vacation with the family. They pray that God will bless them, but they get bent out of shape when somebody else is radically blessed and prosperous. They secretly wish they were radically blessed, yet at the same time, they are quick to point the finger and raise the eyebrows when a pastor or preacher drives a new car, owns a nice house, or goes on a nice vacation. They term this kind of living "excessive," "wasteful," or "irresponsible." They have a certain standard with which to measure a minister's behavior or spending but do not hold themselves to the same standard as a fellow Christian and child of God. Why the double standard? Covetousness, jealousy, and envy are just as sinful and insidious as greed and self-indulgence.

Some people have said to me, "How can we reconcile talking about prosperity with our brothers and sisters in Third World countries who barely have enough?" That's a great question. First, God is who He says He is. Circumstances don't change or define who He is. Second, the socioeconomic conditions are different, not to mention cultural and worldview differences. Prosperity in affluent countries may look like buying a new car or a new house. In a Third World country or agrarian society, it might look like an unexpected bumper crop or harvest, or the birth of ten new calves. You can't compare apples to oranges. Biblical prosperity is not measured by the value of the provision. It is validated simply by the fact that there is no shortfall in God, and that He can provide whenever, however, and whatever.

Some view prosperity as a sign of true spirituality and God's blessings and favor. The prosperity gospel camp gets accused of this. Others think that being poor is a sign of true spirituality because they need to be poor in spirit, not love the world or the things in the world. Neither is true. Money, riches, wealth, and prosperity are neutral in the eyes of God. It is what we do with them that indicates and reflects our spirituality and relationship with Him. Anything taken to extremes is not good. Jesus advocates a prosperity that is attached to kingdom purpose. The blessings and prosperity that God graciously gives us do not have to lead to self-indulgence. Prosperity is not a curse, and is not insidious as some might see it. It's not a dirty word in Christianity.

In the kingdom of God, the purpose of prosperity is twofold. First, to bless the people of God. *"Let them say continually, "Let the* LORD *be magnified, who has pleasure in the prosperity of His servant"* (Psalm 35:27). It brings delight to the Father to see His children blessed. It is only natural and fitting that the Father rejoices when His children are prosperous and successful. He is a good Father. Second, it serves to build and sustain the kingdom of God. God promised Abraham, *"I will make you a great nation; I will bless you and make your name great; and you shall be a blessing"* (Genesis 12:2). To focus and prioritize one purpose over the other is to misrepresent God's heart and intent for His people and kingdom. We are a blessed people, and we are blessed to be a blessing. But it's tough to be a blessing when we don't always have enough.

A WORD ABOUT THE POVERTY SPIRIT

The antithesis of prosperity is poverty or lack. Perhaps we can briefly look back in church history, and discover how poverty became acceptable and was even valued by the church. In the first century church, Gnosticism was rampant—the idea that the material world is evil and only the spirit is good. There was a separation between the physical and the spiritual. They believed that a person cannot be blessed both materially and spiritually. Material possessions, money, and riches were believed to be incompatible with true spirituality.

In the second and third centuries, the church faced great persecution from the Roman Empire. The Christians at that time believed that their sufferings, poverty, and even martyrdom showed and elevated their allegiance and piety to God.

By the fourth century, monasteries were set up in the deserts of Egypt to escape the ways of the world and seek true spirituality. Monks and nuns would live ascetic lives, vowing to live in poverty. Monasticism was likely influenced by the Essenes, who existed during the time of Jesus. They lived beside the Dead Sea and withdrew themselves from society. They subjected themselves to asceticism, taking vows of celibacy and poverty to show their piety to God. The renunciation of worldly material goods was a means of spiritual growth. The phrase "poor in spirit" reflected the way they chose to live.

> ## THE SPIRIT OF POVERTY IS A DISTRUST IN GOD'S GOODNESS.
> ## IT SHINES THE SPOTLIGHT ON SELF-SUFFICIENCY
> ## RATHER THAN GOD'S SUFFICIENCY;
> ## WHAT WE HAVE AND DON'T HAVE VERSUS WHAT GOD HAS.

Thus, we can see why the notion that to be pious is to suffer and be poor was embraced by the early church. It has trickled down through history and continues to affect Christians today. I often hear Christians quoting *"Blessed are the poor in spirit"* (Matthew 5:3) as a sanction to be poor and not enjoy the things of this world. There is a major difference between loving the things of the world and enjoying the things that God blesses us with. One is idolatry; the other is enjoyment and delight. To be poor in spirit is to acknowledge our spiritual bankruptcy. It's a realization of our unworthiness and utter dependence on Him in every area of our lives. This is a far cry from a divine call to be materially or financially poor. It's hard to accept that poverty and lack bring great delight and satisfaction to the Father.

The spirit of poverty is more than lack of money or resources. Some wealthy people have a poverty mind-set, and some poor people have a prosperous mind-set. The orphan spirit (abandonment, isolation, and alienation) and the spirit of poverty are very similar in that they operate from the same root issue—a disconnection and detachment from the love, care, and provision of the Father. The spirit of poverty is a distrust in God's goodness. It shines the spotlight on self-sufficiency rather than God's sufficiency; what we have and don't have versus what God has. It resists and rejects that God has enough to provide for anyone and everyone, anywhere and everywhere, at any time and at the same time! It tries to blind believers to the truth that God is all-sufficient and has unlimited resources, and that, in Him, we are sufficient and have everything. The spirit of poverty is a stronghold that keeps us from living and receiving the fullness of God's plan for our lives. It tries to sabotage the will of God in our lives.

Experiencing lack and having a spirit of lack and poverty are two different things. The difference is the heart motivation. Sometimes, we experience lack, and we have to tighten the belt, and be wise and frugal. The heart learns to be content and focuses on God's grace. (See Philippians 4:11–13.) The spirit of poverty readily admits, "I can't," "There is never enough," "I am not good enough," "God will never come through for me," "I am not worthy of God's goodness." The heart is discontent and focuses on itself.

So how do you know if the spirit of poverty is dogging your heels? The spirit of poverty can rear its ugly head in so many ways and settings in life. Here are twelve ways you could be struggling with the poverty mind-set:

1.   You experience chronic, long-term lack. You often hear yourself complain, "I don't have enough," "I'll never have enough," I'll never be able to pay off my credit card debt."

2.   You envy someone's wealth and riches. You are offended by someone's success and resentful when he or she is getting blessed and not you. You struggle to celebrate other people's victories and breakthroughs.

3.   You are critical about how people spend their money. "I've shared with them my needs. How could they buy that new

car and not help me?" "They spent all that money on that ugly fence. What a waste of money! They should have given it to the church building fund."

4. You cry, "I am never good enough. Poor me!" This is an ugly mind-set that shows up everywhere and in all kinds of settings! It results in insecurity and the fear of man.

5. You live by "it's better to receive than to give." You hate it when the offering bucket comes around. You think it should be banned from church forever. You're stuck with the idea that God is always taking from you but never providing for you.

6. You hoard. It's hard to give things away. When things are handed out for free, you grab as much as possible, even if you don't need them.

7. When you are confronted with an overwhelming situation, you view it as bigger than God.

8. You have a miserly spirit. Generosity is not a trademark of your life. It's not just about finances but your attitude, time, and the way you treat people.

9. Your life is plagued by worry and anxiety. Feelings of joy, peace, and contentment are rare.

10. You believe that you are your own source, not God.

11. You don't think that your pastor should drive a nice car. He needs to remain poor so that he stays humble.

12. You are offended by what I (or anybody) wrote about God's desire for His children to prosper.

The issues surrounding the poverty spirit are complex; I cannot adequately address them in this section alone. Many layers may be involved—psychological, spiritual, cultural and familial, generational, and emotional. Entire books have been written on each of these issues. I pray that the Holy Spirit will help you peel back some of these layers, and grant you understanding, breakthrough, and freedom!

Here are some helpful, practical steps:

1. Pray and invite the Holy Spirit into the process. He will lead you into all truth.

2. Write down and journal about the things He is showing you.

3. Ask Him to show you thought patterns, unhealthy emotions, sinful habits, lies of the enemy, and ways in which you agree with the poverty spirit.

4. Ask Him to show you any hindrances that keep you from receiving the Father's love, blessings, and provision.

5. Repent of anything that He convicts you of.

6. Read books that speak directly into some of the issues He is showing you.

7. Look up and declare Scriptures that speak to who you are, your identity as a child of God, and your unique situations and needs.

8. Process this and pray with somebody you trust.

9. Seek counseling.

10. Find opportunities to praise Him and thank Him for being a generous Provider and Father to you.

"*For as he thinks in his heart, so is he*" (Proverbs 23:7). Our attitudes, speech, and behavior will follow what we believe is true. Jesus said, "*The thief does not come except to steal, and to kill, and to destroy. I have come that they may have life, and that they may have it more abundantly*" (John 10:10). May you uncover the lies the enemy has been using to rob you of God's best. May you see that God has prepared a feast before you, and may you never settle for crumbs under the table.

In addition to eradicating the poverty mind-set, we must pray for wisdom in stewarding His blessings. Many believers have abused the biblical concept of prosperity and have not stewarded it with wisdom. They say something along the lines of, "If God is always going to provide for all my needs when He has unlimited resources, then I will spend my money and resources however and whenever I want." They see it as a license to live recklessly, without wisdom, discipline, and self-control. God does not give us prosperity and blessings without also calling us to live responsibly. Jabez prayed for blessings, and God granted his request. Solomon asked the Lord for wisdom and discernment above riches, and he was blessed with both wisdom and riches. (See 1 Kings 3:5–14.) Wisdom and prosperity go hand in hand. We pray for God's blessings; we must also pray for wisdom to steward the blessings.

> WISDOM AND PROSPERITY GO HAND IN HAND.
> WE PRAY FOR GOD'S BLESSINGS; WE MUST ALSO PRAY FOR
> WISDOM TO STEWARD THE BLESSINGS.

NEVER BOW DOWN TO LACK AGAIN

Jesus taught us to pray, "*Your kingdom come. Your will be done on earth as it is in heaven*" (Matthew 6:10). Our assignment on earth as kingdom ambassadors is to contend in faith for heaven to invade earth until it resembles heaven. There is no lack in heaven. The Father gave us the resources of heaven through Jesus's incarnation. He did not die on the cross for us to serve a tyranny of lack, for that would nullify the very purpose for which He came. Jesus came to establish and prosper the kingdom of God on earth. You and I were never meant to scramble for crumbs under the table. The enemy's sole assignment is to pilfer from the saints of God and rob us of God's provision. Jesus came from heaven to give us abundant life so that we could feast at His table of grace, goodness, and generosity. Now we get to experience and receive from His benevolent nature as the covenant-keeping God and faithful Father.

In this book, I have attempted to give you keys to unlock and access all that God has already made provision for. I am confident that your next provision is around the corner. I am excited for God's radical love to overwhelm you. I wait in eager anticipation to hear the testimonies of His goodness in your life.

May you never bow down to the spirit of lack. May you always feed on His kindness. May His blessings overtake you so that you can be a greater blessing. And may you fulfill your God-given dreams and destiny for the sake of His name and His kingdom.

PRAYER OF FAITH

Thank You, Father, that You do not hide but that reveal Yourself to Your children. You made a way for me to know and experience the nature and fullness of who You are. Give me the spirit of wisdom and understanding to steward Your revelation as *Jehovah Jireh*, the Covenant-Keeper, *El Shaddai*, the All-Sufficient One, in my life. I praise You that You delight in the prosperity of Your children. I declare, from this day forth, prosperity and wholeness will be my portion. Lack and poverty no longer have a hold on me. You are my Father, my Provider, and You will supply all my needs according to Your riches in glory. In Jesus's most magnificent name, I pray. Amen!

ENDNOTES

CHAPTER 1

1. Kenneth A. Mathews, *The New American Commentary*, vol. 1B, *Genesis 11:27–50:26* (Nashville, TN: Broadman & Holman Publishers, 2005), 176.
2. Ray R. Sutton, *That You May Prosper: Dominion by Covenant* (Tyler, TX: Institute for Christian Economics, 1987), 15.
3. Jack W. Hayford, *Spirit Filled Life Bible: New King James Version* (Nashville, TN: Thomas Nelson Publishers, 1991), 27.
4. R. Kent Hughes, *Genesis: Beginning and Blessing*, Preaching the Word (Wheaton, IL: Crossway Books, 2004), 234.
5. Eugene H. Merrill, *The New American Commentary: Deuteronomy*, vol. 4 (Nashville, TN: Broadman & Holman, 1994), 393.
6. Hayford, *Spirit Filled Life Bible*, 29.
7. Sutton, *"That You May Prosper,"* 16.
8. Iain M. Duguid, *Living in the Gap Between Promise and Reality: The Gospel According to Abraham*, *The Gospel According to the Old Testament* (Phillipsburg, N.J.: P & R Publishing Company, 1999), 59.

CHAPTER 2

1. Bruce Wilkinson, *The Prayer of Jabez: Breaking Through to the Blessed Life* (Colorado Springs, CO: Multnomah Publishers, 2000), 19.
2. Wilkinson, *The Prayer of Jabez*, 21.
3. James Strong, "בְּרַךְ," "Hebrew and Aramaic Dictionary of the Old Testament," in *The New Strong's Exhaustive Concordance of the Bible* (Nashville, TN: Thomas Nelson, 2010), 129.

CHAPTER 3

1. Edmond Burke quoted in Edward Parsons Day, comp., *Day's Collacon: An Encyclopedia of Prose Quotations* (New York: International Printing and Publishing Office, 1884), 1013.
2. Michael J. Wilkins, *Matthew: The NIV Application Commentary* (Grand

Rapids, MI: Zondervan, 2004), 292.

3. Ibid., 293.

4. James A. Brooks, *Mark*, The New American Commentary, vol. 23, (Nashville, TN: Broadman Press, 1991), 165.

5. R. T. France, *The Gospel of Mark: The New International Greek Testament Commentary* (Grand Rapids, MI: William B. Eerdmans Publishing Company, 2002), 408.

6. James R. Edwards, *The Gospel According to Mark: The Pillar New Testament Commentary* (Grand Rapids, MI: William B. Eerdmans Publishing Company, 2002), 317.

7. Wilkins, *Matthew: The NIV Application Commentary*, 293.

8. Billy Graham quoted in Richard D. Allen, *The Genesis Principle of Leadership: Claiming and Cultivating Your Created Capacity* (Mustang, OK: Tate Publishing and Enterprises, 2008), 221.

9. R. T. France, *The Gospel According to Matthew: An Introduction and Commentary*, The Tyndale New Testament Commentaries (Leicester, England: Inter-Varsity Press, 1985), 138.

10. Ibid.

11. Craig S. Keener, *A Commentary on the Gospel of Matthew* (Grand Rapids, MI: William B. Eerdmans Publishing Company, 1999), 232.

12. Robert H. Mounce, *Matthew: New International Biblical Commentary* (Peabody, MA: Hendrickson Publishers, 1991), 60.

13. Ronald F. Youngblood, ed., *Nelson's New Illustrated Bible Dictionary* (Nashville, TN: Thomas Nelson, 1995), 794.

14. Gerhard Kittel and Gerhard Friedrich, eds., *Theological Dictionary of the New Testament: Abridged in One Volume* (Grand Rapids, MI: William B. Eerdmans Publishing Company, 1985), 552.

15. Ibid.

16. Keener, *A Commentary on the Gospel of Matthew*, 233.

CHAPTER 4

1. Robert H. Mounce quoted in Joe Carter, *NIV Lifehacks Bible: Practical Tools for Successful Spiritual Habits* (Grand Rapids, MI: Zondervan, 2015).

2. Donald A. Hagner, *Word Biblical Commentary: Matthew 1–13*, vol. 33a (Dallas, TX: Word Incorporated, 1993), 163.

3. Craig S. Keener, *Matthew*, The IVP New Testament Commentary Series (Downers Grove, IL: InterVarsity Press, 1997), 153.

4. Hagner, *Word Biblical Commentary: Matthew 1–13*, 164.

5. Winston Churchill quoted in Ken Harrington and Jeanne Harrington, *Deliverance from Toxic Memories: Weapons to Overcome Destructive Thought Patterns in Your Life* (Shippensburg, PA: Destiny Image Publishers, 2013).

6. Hagner, *Word Biblical Commentary: Matthew 1–13*, 165–166.

7. Frederick Dale Bruner, *Matthew: A Commentary*, rev. and exp. ed., vol. 1 (Grand Rapids, MI: William B. Eerdmans, 2004), 333–334.

8. Johann Tauler quoted in Michael Green, *The Message of Matthew* (Downers Grove, IL: InterVarsity Press, 2000).

CHAPTER 5

1. T. Desmond Alexander and Brian S. Rosner, *New Dictionary of Biblical Theology* (Downers Grove, IL: InterVarsity Press, 2000), 377.
2. Norman C. Gore. *Tzeenah U-Reenah: A Jewish Commentary on the Book of Exodus* (New York: Vantage Press, 1965), 134.
3. Umberto Cassuto, *A Commentary on the Book of Exodus* (Jerusalem: Magnes Press, 1974), 246.

CHAPTER 6

1. Mother Teresa, *Love: A Fruit Always in Season, Daily Meditations by Mother Teresa* (San Francisco, CA: Ignatius Press, 1987), 118.
2. John I. Durham, *Word Biblical Commentary: Exodus*, vol. 3 (Waco, TX: Word Incorporated, 1987), 38.
3. James R. Edwards, *The Gospel According to Luke*, The Pillar New Testament Commentary (Grand Rapids, MI: W.B. Eerdmans, 2015), 338.
4. Frederick W. Danker, *Jesus and the New Age: A Commentary on St. Luke's Gospel* (Philadelphia: Fortress Press, 1988), 231.

CHAPTER 7

1. Joni Eareckson Tada quoted in Randy Alcorn, *Happiness* (Carol Stream, IL: NavPress, 2015).
2. Luisa Kroll, "Forbes 2016 World's Billionaires: Meet the Richest People on the Planet," *Forbes* (1 March 2016), https://www.forbes.com/sites/luisakroll/2016/03/01/forbes-2016-worlds-billionaires-meet-the-richest-people-on-the-planet/#6780255c77dc.
3. Gerald F. Hawthorne, *Word Biblical Commentary: Philippians*, vol. 43 (Dallas, TX: Word Incorporated, 1993), 206.
4. Frank Thielman, *Philippians: The NIV Application Commentary* (Grand Rapids, MI: Zondervan, 1995), 237.
5. Hawthorne, *Word Biblical Commentary: Philippians*, 207.

CHAPTER 8

1. Virginia Whitman quoted in Charlie Jones and Bob Kelly, *The Tremendous Power of Prayer* (West Monroe, LA: Howard Publishing Company, 2000), 93–94.
2. Ceslas Spicq, *Theological Lexicon of the New Testament*, ed. and trans. James D. Ernest, vol. 3 (Peabody, MA: Hendrickson Publishers, 1994), 421.
3. William L. Lane, *Word Biblical Commentary: Hebrews 9–13*, vol. 47b (Dallas, TX: Word Incorporated, 1993), 329.
4. Philip Edgcumbe Hughes, *A Commentary on the Epistle to the Hebrews* (Grand Rapids, MI: William B. Eerdmans, 1977), 440–441.
5. Arthur S. Peake, *Heroes and Martyrs of Faith* (London: Hodder and Stoughton, 1910), 12.
6. Robert H. Stein, *Mark: Baker Exegetical Commentary on the New Testament* (Grand Rapids, MI: Baker Academic, 2008), 520.

CHAPTER 9

1. Thielman, *Philippians: The NIV Application Commentary*, 236.

CHAPTER 10

1. Suzanne Woolley, "Do You Have More Debt Than the Average American?" Bloomberg (15 December 2016), https://www.bloomberg.com/news/articles/2016-12-15/average-credit-card-debt-16k-total-debt-133k-where-do-you-fit-in.

CHAPTER 11

1. Allen P. Ross, *Creation and Blessing: A Guide to the Study and Exposition of the Book of Genesis* (Grand Rapids, MI: Baker Book House, 1988), 400.
2. Gordon J. Wenham, *Word Bible Commentary: Genesis 1–15*, vol. 1 (Nashville, TN: Thomas Nelson, 1987), 316.
3. Wenham, *Word Bible Commentary: Genesis 1–15*, 324.
4. James Strong, *The New Strong's Exhaustive Concordance of the Bible* (Nashville, TN: Thomas Nelson, 2010), 88.

ABOUT THE AUTHOR

Founder of 7K and Elisha's Room, Dr. Cornelius Quek was born into a Buddhist family in Singapore. Even at a young age, he had an acute sense of spirituality. At sixteen years old, he encountered the love of Jesus, and his life was dramatically transformed. He was radically saved and delivered from temple and pagan idol worship. His father, out of sheer anger and desperation, sought out a temple medium, or fortune teller, to inquire about Cornelius. The temple medium told his father, "The Spirit that is on him, I have no power to touch." Many years later, he experienced the great joy of leading his parents to the Lord.

Cornelius received his theological training from London School of Theology in the United Kingdom. He also earned master of divinity and doctor of ministry degrees from the world-renowned Oral Roberts University, researching the ministry of the supernatural in the marketplace. He is a fruit of Oral Roberts University's ministry to take God's healing power into every man's world.

Cornelius is passionate about speaking to, equipping, and mentoring contemporary leaders and culture-makers to influence every sphere of society. He and his beautiful wife, Tiffany, have been commissioned by Bethel Church in Redding, California. He also teaches at Bethel Church and at the Bethel School of Supernatural Ministry.

For more information about the ministry of Dr. Cornelius Quek, visit:

The7K.org

Welcome to Our House!

We Have a Special Gift for You

It is our privilege and pleasure to share in your love of Christian books. We are committed to bringing you authors and books that feed, challenge, and enrich your faith.

To show our appreciation, we invite you to sign up to receive a specially selected **Reader Appreciation Gift**, with our compliments. Just go to the Web address at the bottom of this page.

God bless you as you seek a deeper walk with Him!

WE HAVE A GIFT FOR YOU. VISIT:

whpub.me/nonfictionthx

WHITAKER
HOUSE